Planning and Building Your Fireplace

Margaret and Wilbur F. Eastman

GARDEN WAY PUBLISHING
CHARLOTTE VERMONT

To Santa Claus,
who, more than anyone else, has
popularized fireplaces, especially
those with clean flues that do not soil
his red suit and white beard
when he is convected back up the
chimney on his merry rounds

Diagrams by Horace Gilmore
Chapter opening illustrations by Paula Savastano
Line art by Ralph Scott
Designed by Bruce Williamson

Printed in the United States

ISBN: 0-88266-083-7 (paperback)
       0-88266-084-5 (hardcover)

Fourth Printing, February 1978

Contents

Introduction

Interest in fireplaces is growing, and with that growth is an increase in the questions about them.

Those who are building homes have practical questions: What is the most energy-efficient fireplace? Where shall we put the fireplace? How much will it cost? Is it too big a job for us to do ourselves? Where can we find a reliable mason?

And among homeowners there is another common question: What causes this fireplace to smoke, and is there anything we can do about it?

This book is written to answer these questions, and many more.

There is a "mystique" about fireplace construction. We will attempt to penetrate this mystique and to set forth sound, basic principles of building a fireplace — one that will give off the maximum amount of heat without smoking. These principles (basically very simple) are based on the scientific research of Count Rumford. We shall have much to say about Rumford, for he discovered what makes a fireplace efficient and what sends smoke up the chimney rather than out into the room.

We'll start off by discussing what one may expect from a fireplace in terms of heat. How efficient is a good fireplace? How can that efficiency be improved? Is a fireplace a satisfactory home-heating system? Or is a good stove better? And we will have something to say about the romantic side of having a fireplace.

Then we'll dissect a fireplace and chimney to learn what the various components are, what they are designed to do, what their relationship is with other parts of the fireplace.

We shall also discuss the best location for a fireplace. What are the important considerations? Then how is it built? What about problems of weight? What size footings? What about the style? And where does one locate the hearth? How much will it cost?

So often when one thinks about a fireplace, one thinks only of the opening into the chimney and the dancing flames. But one must never forget the chimney — the all-important chimney. Just as beautiful music may be ruined by a poor speaker system, so may a beautiful fireplace be disappointing if an improper chimney has been built.

A properly constructed fireplace and chimney should not result in a fireplace that smokes; for those who inherited a house with a fireplace that smokes, we'll have a summary chapter about how to make a fireplace draw properly.

There are many improvizations on the market today related to fireplaces. These include Franklin stoves, heatsavers, modified fireplaces, and numerous inventions to extract more heat from the fireplace. These will be discussed so that the reader can decide whether or not they are for him.

It has been said that a fireplace is no better than the fuel it burns. Fuel is important, and we'll discuss the various types of fuels most commonly used and their efficiencies.

Nor will we neglect to discuss fireplace accessories and preventive maintenance of the fireplace and chimney. The common chimney sweep who brightened many a children's book with his black-smudged smile is not available anymore, but there are many things the homeowner can and should do to keep the chimney clear of soot.

The chapter of fireplace designs may prove useful to those who are contemplating adding a fireplace to their home, for these designs should give some clue to the way a fireplace will influence the appearance of a room or living area.

And finally there is a chapter on sources of information relating to fireplaces and fireplace building, places where you may write for information and for supplies.

MCE
WFE

1 How Efficient is a Fireplace?

When one stands before a blazing fireplace and feels its warmth, it is difficult to be other than enthusiastic about fireplaces. This masks the fact that they are very inefficient as heaters, since approximately 90 percent of the heat from the flames goes up the chimney. And the heat one feels on one's front stops right there, leaving one's back still cold. Furthermore, much of the warmth already in the room escapes up the chimney when the fireplace is burning (and even more continues to escape up the chimney when the fire is out unless the damper is closed). Unless the fire has good access to air (oxygen), which it needs to keep burning, it will create drafts by pulling outside air into the room through cracks in doors and windows. Lack of enough air (often indicating a well-built, well-insulated house) will cause the fire to die and smoke to escape into the room.

HOW MUCH HEAT?

Even with the present-day modifications to improve its usefulness as a heating source, the fireplace is not as efficient as either a stove or a furnace. If you are thinking of a fireplace as a primary source of heat, you might do well to think twice and perhaps settle on some other form of heater. It has been estimated that as the sole source of heat for the home, a fireplace will require up to four times as much wood as is required by a modern wood-burning stove.

But heat may not be the only reason to have a fireplace. Certainly its presence lends a great deal of enchantment and coziness to a room. It is a symbol of friendship and hospitality. In many homes it is the family center, and its brilliant dancing flames create a romantic atmosphere difficult to achieve in any other way. It has its own language which every age can understand. And this alone may well be worth your investment. Certainly a fireplace will add more than its cost to the value of your home.

The fireplace also has great possibilities for improving the appearance of a room, and its wide variety of design may be used to accent particular motifs. Interior decorators favor it as an indoor welcome mat to draw guests toward a common focal point.

But to understand fully just how a fireplace does, and does not, contribute to heat efficiency, we need to understand how heat is moved from the fire to various other places and how it may be used most efficiently to warm cold surfaces. This is basic to the understanding of building a successful and efficient fireplace.

Transfer of Heat

There are three fundamental ways heat may be transferred from one place to another: by radiation, by conduction, and by convection.

If you are outside on a bright and clear winter day and the sun strikes your face, your face will feel warm even though the air around you may be very cold. Only your face and those surfaces of your body that are struck by the sun's rays feel its warmth. Your back does not, and your feet are still cold. That is because heat from the sun is being transferred to your face by radiation (direct rays from the sun hitting you). The air between you and the sun is not heated. A thermometer in direct sunlight will indicate a temperature well above the temperature of the surrounding air.

So it is with heat from the fire when it comes out into the room from the fireplace. This is radiant heat, and it warms

"Fireside enjoyments and home-born happiness."

Cowper

2

only surfaces it strikes directly; it does not heat the air between the fireplace and the surfaces it strikes.

A simple experiment will illustrate. Stand in front of a fireplace with the fireplace screen closed; then suddenly open the screen and notice how much more heat strikes you. This is because many of the heat rays from the fire were stopped by the wire surfaces of the screen.

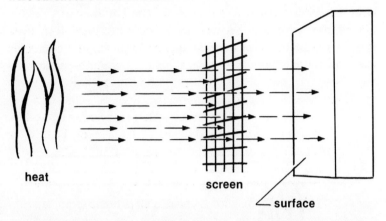

heat   screen

surface

The direct transfer of heat from one surface to another is conduction. If you put the fire tongs on the embers, the tongs will become hot directly from the fire the same way your finger will become hot, and possibly burned, if you put it directly on a hot electric iron. Once the back masonry wall of the fireplace, for instance, becomes hot, the heat in the masonry will transfer itself to other areas of the solid masonry that are not as hot; this occurs by direct transfer. Perhaps you have noticed that after a fire has been burning for a while in a fireplace whose back wall forms the partition of another room, you can feel the heat coming through the masonry in the second room. The heat comes through because that wall is in direct contact with the masonry that already is hot. It helps to think of heat transfer by conduction as transfer by "touching."

"A fireplace supplies radiant energy that can bring quick comfort to a cold room. In spring and fall, a fire will dispel early morning and evening chills more economically than a large heating system, since less fuel is consumed and a large volume of heat is quickly produced. Should storms or power failures interrupt the normally reliable means of heating and cooking, it is reassuring to have a fireplace for emergency use."

USDA Leaflet 559,
Firewood for Your Fireplace

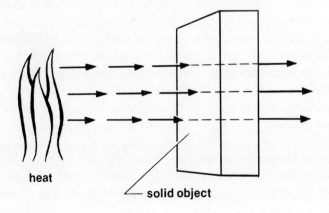

heat

solid object

The third method of heat transfer is convection. This is the transfer of heat from one place to another via the movement of a fluid, such as water or air (if you are willing to think of air as a "fluid" for the purpose of this discussion). As air moves, it picks up heat directly (by conduction) from the surfaces it touches; accordingly the air is heated, and the temperature in the room will rise as the air gains this heat. Hot air rises, and cold air falls. The heat that goes up the chimney after air is heated by the coals in the fireplace is convected heat. Radiators heat by convection, for moving air picks up heat and circulates it to warm the room.

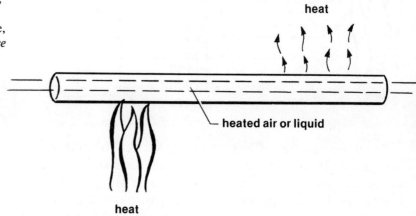

heat

heated air or liquid

heat

For thousands of years man has been involved with fire for heat and cooking. Over these years he has developed ways to increase its efficiency. And even today he is still fascinated by the problem.

HISTORY OF THE FIREPLACE

The development of the fireplace took place primarily in cold, damp climates. People in the British Isles, especially, and northern Europe have contributed much to its history, as have those who lived in the colder areas of America.

The English fireplaces of the fifth and sixth centuries were open, often with raised hearths, placed in the middle of the great halls for maximum radiation. Although these fireplaces were depended upon for heating and cooking, they were far from being efficient, and smoke rising from the fires often failed to find a way out in spite of roof openings for that purpose.

By the sixteenth century, the open fireplace gave way to the metal or masonry hooded fireplace set against the wall and vented through to the outside for smoke removal. This became necessary when the Normans began building two-story houses, which no longer made the hole in the roof feasible. The development of chimneys of various designs and styles soon followed. The fireplaces, too, were modified. Some were designed with seats almost within the fireplace opening where one might sit to keep warm. The Scandinavians built corner fireplaces with raised hearths and huge stone hoods to absorb heat and to release it gradually. These fireplaces sometimes were set out from the wall to enable people to walk behind them to keep warm.

When wood became scarce in England, coal was substituted, and smaller fireplaces were built so heat would not be wasted. During the twelfth to the sixteenth centuries, fireplaces and chimneys were embellished with period architectural styles and materials. The development and improvement of cast iron, for instance, encouraged many to use ornate castings for the backs and sides of fireplaces, especially in the fifteenth and sixteenth centuries. Iron fireplace accessories also came into use.

When settlers came to America from England, they continued to use the fireplace for heating and cooking. Since these colonists had learned that masonry fireplaces absorb heat and release it slowly, they built fireplaces of brick and fieldstone in the center of the house to provide warmth for the rooms. Some of these fires never went out from year to year.

Coal Substituted

"An English farmer in America, who makes great fires in large open chimneys (fireplaces), needs the constant employment of one man to cut and haul wood for supplying them; and the draft of cold air to them is so strong, that the heels of his family are frozen, while they are scorching their faces, and the room is never warm, so that little sedentary work can be done by them in winter."

Benjamin Franklin,
*On the Causes and Cure
of Smoky Chimneys*

The Vermont House parlor at the Shelburne (Vt.) Museum.

5

Their fireplaces often had separate ovens built into the same masonry unit. These ovens were filled with live coals to heat the surrounding masonry. When the coals were raked out, bread or meat was put in. Then the oven was closed tightly to allow the food to cook from the absorbed heat. Later, the ovens were modified to provide for a separate firebox underneath with its own vent outside or into the main chimney. Other types of ovens were made of metal and were placed directly on the main hearth for baking.

At best these fireplaces were inefficient, and the drafts they created made the winged chair popular. (This is a fireside chair with wing-like projections at face level to protect the occupant from drafts across his face.)

Stoves Become Popular

"A fireplace is an inefficient heater, a fire hazard, a source of smelly gases, a dust catcher, and a general domestic nuisance. Its chimney sucks already-heated air out of a room like a vacuum cleaner, its ash dump always seems full, and it is possessed of a perverse individuality that sees it react to every ounce of barometric pressure, knot of wind or degree of temperature. You can never cut enough wood to satisfy its voracious appetite, and you must maintain an enormous larder of twigs, shavings, paper and assorted sizes of seasoned wood to satiate its finicky palate. The fireplace loads the ground with too much weight, it tends to settle unevenly, and its building requires an inordinate amount of construction time, money and patience. A fireplace is like a child: It is difficult to conceive, expensive to feed, and has trouble supporting itself in old age. In short, there is no rational reason for wanting a fireplace.

"But what is a stone house without one?"

Karl and Sue Schwenke,
Build Your Own Stone House

Soon after 1800 when the "enclosed" stove was introduced, there was a sharp decrease in the use of the fireplace. From 1850 until the twentieth century, the cast iron stove was most popular. The enclosed stove had the advantage of a draft that could be regulated to provide the amount of air needed to burn the gases released by the fire and at the same time feed the fire itself.

Following the advent of the enclosed stove, the furnace was developed to provide central heating. The first fuel was wood, but later developments, like those for the stove, allowed coal, oil, and gas to be substituted.

In recent years the fireplace has become popular again. People not only recognized its esthetic qualities and the spirit of cheerfulness it generates, but also are concerned about the energy crisis. For this reason many returned to wood heat (when that fuel is available) which has brought back the use of the wood stove.

Since a conventional fireplace is less heat-efficient than a stove, various attempts have been made to modify the fireplace. Many inventions have resulted. These include metal pre-built units around which masonry is laid to allow air to circulate and transfer heat from the masonry to the room. Masonry modifications without such pre-built units are also common. Circulating-water lines, hollow grate-irons with fans, and countless other ways are being used to capture and circulate heat.

Earlier attempts also were made. Records tell of a French doctor, Louis Savot, who experimented, rather crudely, with circulating heat from a fireplace in the early 1600's.

The person generally credited with being the most successful in such early attempts is Benjamin Franklin. In 1744 he published a pamphlet describing the Pennsylvanian Fireplace which he invented and which is recognized as the first successful heat-circulating fireplace.

Franklin, with his inquisitive mind, was concerned with many things — electricity, politics, travel, good eating, international relations, and on and on. But what could have intrigued him about fireplaces? No doubt he spent many hours in conferences and being entertained before roaring fires, wondering why he never got warm and why there always was so much smoke in the room.

In 1784, while en route home from Paris, he gave much thought to the matter of smoky fireplaces as he sat out the long voyage. During the trip he wrote his friend in Vienna, Dr. Jan Ingenhousz. The letter was published shortly thereafter with the title, "On the Causes and Cure of Smoky Chimneys." (Franklin referred to fireplaces as "chimneys" and what we call chimneys, he called "funnels.")

In his letter to Ingenhousz, Franklin proposed nine reasons why fireplaces smoke, and suggested ways to correct them. He contended that the only way smoke can get up a chimney is to be carried by heat, since smoke is heavier than air, and suggested ways this could be provided. He also argued against large fireplaces, believing they wasted heat and were prone to smoke.

Ben Franklin

"A second cause of the smoking of chimneys (fireplaces) is, their openings in the room being too large; that is, too wide, too high, or both. . . . If you suspect that your chimney (fireplace) smokes from the too great dimension of its opening, contract it by placing movable boards so as to lower and narrow it gradually, till you find the smoke no longer issues into the room. The proportion so found will be that which is proper for that chimney, and you may employ the bricklayer or mason to reduce it accordingly."

Benjamin Franklin,
On the Causes and Cure of Smoky Chimneys

The Pennsylvanian Fireplace. While hundreds of these were built in Franklin's day, this is the only known unit still in existence. From the collection of the Mercer Museum of the Bucks County Historical Association.

7

Count Rumford

The person now credited with doing more than anyone else to perfect the design of the fireplace is Count Rumford, a contemporary of Franklin.

He was born Benjamin Thompson in Woburn, Mass., in 1753. He, too, was a genius in his time although he was not recognized as such in America until quite recently. His life was unusual indeed. He was known as a Tory by his neighbors since he maintained allegiance to King George III. He was a friend of the royal governor of New Hampshire, John Wentworth, whom Thompson met after he married a widow from Rumford (now Concord), N. H. General Gage of the British Army in Massachusetts sent Thompson to London to deliver a message to the secretary of state for the colonies, and while in London, Thompson became the latter's private secretary. Soon he rose to become under-secretary of state for the colonies and was knighted. Somewhat later he met the reigning monarch of Bavaria, who conferred on him the title of count, and Thompson, remembering his wife's birthplace in New Hampshire, took the title of Count Rumford.

Rumford's exploits in Bavaria were many and so extraordinary that he was named minister to the Court of St. James and a general in the army. He received numerous accolades in England and in Bavaria, and the elite among the politicians and scientists of these countries were well known to him.

His scientific mind was in constant motion. When in Bavaria, he sought to improve the army's capability to move supplies, its arms, the nutritional content of its food and its tactical efficiency. His interests also included improving the efficiency of the household kitchen and the breeds of farm animals.

Eventually, however, Count Rumford returned to England where he became concerned with fireplaces; why they smoked, and what could be done to improve their heat output and to reduce fuel consumption. He studied more than 500 fireplaces, rebuilt many of them, and had fireplaces built to his own design. From this study he formulated principles that solved many of the heat and smoke problems. The principles stand today as solid and scientific, and Count Rumford is best remembered for this part of his illustrious career.

Probably few if any of his contemporaries had so many high titles and from so many different European countries as did Count Rumford. Today, however, we think of him as the forgotten American who did more than anyone else to improve the efficiency of the fireplace. He understood that heat is transmitted by motion, that heat thrown off by a fireplace is radiant heat, and that radiant heat does not heat the air. His correction of many faulty fireplaces was predicated upon this knowledge.

The fireplace has gone from not much more than an open camp fire to the greatly changed fireplaces we see today in so many variations — conventional, modified, and free-standing, for example — and in between we see its history and development being interrupted by attention to stoves and furnaces of various kinds. But as we scan its long history, we notice that these many developments have resulted from man's attempt to find a more efficient way to bring heat into the room and to eliminate smoke. Somewhere above all this we note that man has placed a high degree of importance on the romantic atmosphere a fireplace brings to the home.

Heat, decoration, romance — it is against all these that one has to decide if indeed he really wants to invest in a fireplace.

Cleaning the stones of this huge fireplace is one of the last steps before completion.

2 Component Parts of a Fireplace

It is much simpler to describe how something is done if we name the various parts. And it is even better if we know what these parts look like and how they work.

So let's take a look at the fireplace and its chimney just to become acquainted with their various components. So much of what makes up a fireplace and a chimney is hidden inside the wall that it is easy to overlook the units that make up the entire assembly. Accordingly, when we dissect the assembly, we find that it is not just an opening for a fire with a smoke outlet but rather a more involved structure.

Let's start by looking at the front of a common, ordinary fireplace.

As we face the fireplace, we see a large rectangular opening in the wall, and this is indeed called the *fireplace opening*. The sizes of the fireplace openings vary a great deal, depending on factors we shall discuss later. In addition, they vary architecturally, depending on the style of the fireplace, which usually is integrated with the decor of the room.

Around the sides and top of the fireplace opening is the *facing*. Facing probably should be thought of as a sort of veneer that hides the rough masonry of the fireplace to give it a finished look. Often the facing is of the same kind of masonry as the exterior of the chimney (stone, brick), but ceramic tile and other masonry materials are also used. Even metal facings are not uncommon; in fact, they were quite fashionable when cast iron was first used. Because the facing is so close to the fire itself, it must be of noncombustible material; and frequently local building codes will mandate what should, or should not, be used. Often facing will have a wide outer molding, or *frame*, around it, and this should always be at least six inches from the inside edge of the facing to prevent its being set afire.

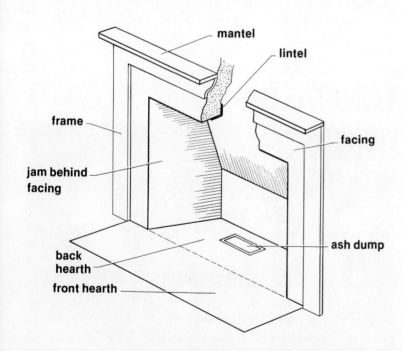

"Shut in from all the world without
Content to let the northwind roar."

Whittier,
Snowbound

11

FIREPLACE JAMBS

Behind the facing on the sides of the fireplace opening are the *jambs*. These add support to the fireplace, and their width is frequently determined with an eye to decor and style. Twelve to sixteen inches in width is usual.

If you look closely at the underside of the facing that goes across the top of the fireplace opening, you may see that a heavy metal angle iron has been used as support for the masonry above this opening. This is the *lintel*, and it extends into the jambs for sound anchoring. Sometimes lintels are large stone slabs that extend over the fireplace opening and rest their ends in the masonry behind the facing. Occasionally an actual masonry arch will substitute for the lintel as the support for the weight of the masonry above the opening; in such instances the jambs must be strong enough to support the thrust of the arch. The most common kind of lintel used today is the heavy angle iron; most masonry supply houses carry metal lintels as common stock items.

THE MANTEL

Above the facing on top of the fireplace opening a *mantel* is usually found. Mantels are often made of wood, but stone and brick are also common. Generally a mantel is thought of as a shelf. Some fireplaces have no mantels; others have a heavy or rather ornate molding that is only reminiscent of a shelf. The type of mantel is strictly a matter of the decorator's taste when the fireplace is built. Mantels have no function other than dec-

This modern fireplace unit, a Majestic Thulman fireplace, features a mantel that blends well with the decor of this room.

oration and simple utility, but they should always be at least 12 inches above the top of the fireplace opening as a precaution against fire hazards.

Other mantels are really not mantels at all but are parts of the frames around the sides and top of the opening. Convention still lets us refer to them as mantels.

Lumber yards and masonry supply houses carry mantles in a wide variety of styles.

Inside the fireplace opening is, of course, the floor of the fireplace. This is called the *hearth*. The hearth should extend outside of the fireplace into the room at least 20 inches, in which case that part inside the fireplace is known as the *back hearth* and that part outside is known as the *front hearth*. You will recognize the back hearth as being the area over which the fire is built. The front hearth protects that area of the room from possible fire caused by sparks shooting out from the fireplace opening.

"Now stir the fire, and close the
    shutters fast,
Let fall the curtains,
    wheel the sofa round,
And, while the bubbling and
    loud-hissing urn
Throws up a steamy column,
    and the cups,
That cheer but not inebriate,
    wait on each,
So let us welcome
    peaceful ev'ning in."

William Cowper,
The Winter Evening

We often hear people speak of *raised hearths,* which simply means the floor of the fireplace (the hearth) is above the level of the floor of the room. When this is the situation, the front hearth is usually raised as well, and sometimes it is broadened to the right and left to be almost a seat by the fireplace or a storage place for small amounts of wood.

If you look toward the rear of the back hearth, you may see a small metal cover, which, upon closer examination, will prove to be a sort of door on a metal hinge. This is the *ash dump,* which makes it easy to get rid of ashes by raking them into the *ash pit,* underneath. We'll encounter the matter of the ash pit again when we see how the ashes are finally removed from the house.

Now let's take a look at the back and sides of the inside of the fireplace opening, better known as the *fire chamber.*

The lower part of its rear wall appears to be vertical, but less than half-way up it suddenly makes a slight bend (not a curve) forward. This entire back is known as the *fireback,* but it is better if this term is used to refer only to the lower part which is vertical; the slanting part is then referred to as *the slope of the fireback.* The sides, which are at obtuse angles from the rear wall, are called *covings.* Firebacks, slopes of firebacks, and covings should be made of *firebrick* (a brick not to be confused with common building brick, the latter being used for fireplace facings and chimneys).

RAISED HEARTHS

The covings are joined at the front of the fireplace opening with, and become part of, the jambs.

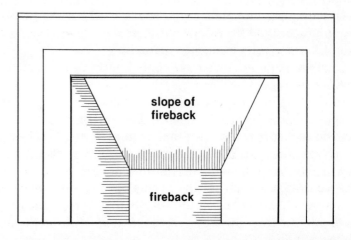

slope of fireback

fireback

METAL PARTS

In some fireplaces, especially those built in the eighteenth century, the fireback and covings were of metal.

Let's take another look at some of the parts we have mentioned thus far. But instead of looking at them from a front elevation, we'll look at them in a cross-section.

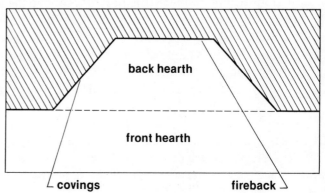

back hearth

front hearth

covings   **fireback**

And on the following page a still different look; this time a side elevation from the foundation up to where the fireplace joins the chimney.

Masonry fireplaces and chimneys must have foundation support, and today most have their own separate foundations or *footing* regardless of whether they are completely within the house or whether the chimney is on the outside. These footings support the entire fireplace and chimney structure. From the outside we see only the masonry coming up from the ground, but underneath there is a foundation of reinforced concrete which is considerably larger than the length and width of the chimney itself in order to give adequate support.

Keep in mind that fireplaces and chimneys should not support any of the weight of the house — none whatsoever. In other words, no support beams of the house should rest on any part of the fireplace or chimney masonry. It is said that a fireplace should "float" insofar as the house is concerned. The reason for this is simple: Should the house settle, or should the fireplace and chimney settle (God forbid!), the masonry will be subject to cracks, misalignment, and possible permanent damage.

Next, look at the back hearth with the opening we referred to as the ash dump. Notice that underneath, the masonry has been laid to provide a hollow space for the ashes. This is called the *ash pit*. And the ashes may be cleaned out via the door to the ash pit. In the illustration the door to the ash pit is in the basement of the home; however, the door could just as well have been on the other side of the chimney if that side happened to be outside the house. The ash pit and its door are a convenience. For otherwise, the ashes and dust would have to be removed directly from the hearth. The size of the ash pit and the frequency with which the fireplace is used determine how often the ash pit requires cleaning out, but it should never be left until it is full of ashes. Ashes have a tendency to become damp, to settle, and to "hardpan," which makes the removal job difficult if it is postponed too long. It also is best to rake only cool ashes into the ash pit — never coals which could perhaps find an outlet for smoke and sparks if the masonry is not completely tight.

Notice in the illustration how the front hearth comes right out to butt against the framing of the floor. This would be the same whether the hearth were raised or not.

It is difficult in this illustration to show the coving and the angle where it joins the fireback, but we do see the lintel. Above the lintel is the *breast,* masonry that connects the front of the fireplace with the chimney.

Above the breast we find the *flue.* A flue is actually a passage for smoke and gases within a larger structure we call the chimney. Each flue should be linked to only one fire source. For example, it could be linked with the fireplace, or the incinerator, or the kitchen stove, or the furnace, but not more than one of them, to avoid problems of improper draft. A chimney may well have more than one flue in it (one for the downstairs fire-

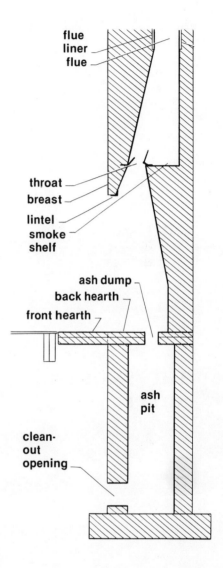

**SUPPORT
NO WEIGHT**

flue
liner
flue

throat
breast
lintel
smoke
shelf

ash dump
back hearth
front hearth

ash
pit

clean-
out
opening

**ONE FLUE
PER FIRE**

place, one for the upstairs fireplace, and one for the furnace, for instance). Some have tried having a common flue for two or more fire sources, but it is a matter of pure luck if this is successful. It most definitely is not to be encouraged, and most building codes forbid it.

Building codes usually require flues to have *flue liners* — lengths of vitrified fire clay, the walls of which are a minimum of five-eighths of an inch thick. These liners are made to withstand sudden changes in temperature as well as the action of flue gases which would otherwise cause chimney bricks to disintegrate slowly, thereby causing fire hazards and reducing the effectiveness of drafts. Many older homes do not have flue liners, and when chimney fires occur, the consequences are often extremely serious. If a chimney fire occurs when flue liners are used, there is seldom any problem or danger if the liners have been properly installed. They also are strong enough to withstand the terrific pressure exerted by a fire as it seeks an outlet in a narrow passageway. Liners come in various lengths and with various size openings. They may be rectangular, square, or round.

THE SMOKE SHELF

"Golden lads and girls all must,
As chimney-sweepers, come to dust."

Shakespeare,
Cymbeline

At the bottom of the flue you will notice a shelf that juts out into the flue. This is a *smoke shelf,* and it is an extremely important component of a successful fireplace. This invention of Count Rumford will be discussed later in this chapter.

Opposite the smoke shelf is a narrow opening to the breast. This is known as the *throat* — another very important part of the fireplace which Count Rumford improved by narrowing it from its previous size to 3-4 inches in width.

Why was it so wide before? Because it had to be wide enough for chimney sweeps to send small boys up to clean out the flue. Now there are other and better ways to clean a flue. And the narrower throat has made the fireplace much more efficient.

It is quite common to think of the throat and the *damper* as one and the same thing. Most fireplaces these days have dampers, and the damper, a metal unit running the entire width of the fireplace opening, can be adjusted from in front of the fireplace to various size openings as needed to increase the efficiency of the up-draft. Think of the damper as an adjustable metal unit sitting on top of the throat, both of which are as long as the fireplace opening is wide.

16

Dampers come in various stock sizes and are built into the fireplace masonry as the masonry is laid up.

Another good reason for the damper is that it may be partially shut to lessen the amount of heat loss from the room up the chimney, or it may be closed completely when the fireplace is not in use.

We once had a family of raccoons spend a summer on the smoke shelf in our fireplace, and it was only the closed damper that prevented them from coming out into the living room. Our neighbors were not so fortunate. They found raccoons romping in their living room one morning when they came downstairs for breakfast. Squirrels also enjoy investigating chimneys, and they can be most destructive if they enter a room through an open damper.

Another perspective of the fireplace may be helpful here, for it shows how the damper is situated and that its length is the same as the width of the fireplace opening. The illustration also indicates how, above the damper, the opening is gradually reduced and tapered to lead nicely and smoothly into the fireplace flue. This area where the opening is reduced is frequently referred to as the *smoke chamber.*

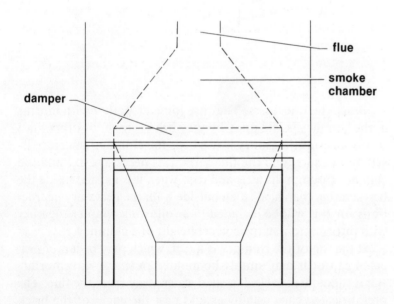

NO
OUTCROPPINGS

Notice, too, that everywhere the smoke and flames travel, their conduits are smooth and without jagged edges or outcroppings. Jagged conduits cause the smoke to build up soot and clog the passageways; trouble compounds trouble until the fireplace becomes very inefficient and chances of chimney fires are great. Nothing should be done to impede the rapid and complete passage of smoke and gases up the chimney.

Let's go to the chimney now, and this time to concentrate on that part that encloses the flue or flues.

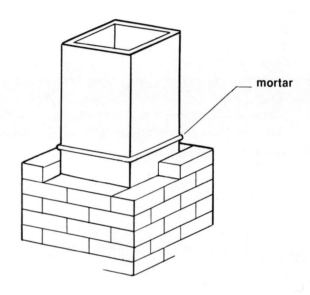

mortar

"Billy, in one of his nice new sashes,
Fell in the fire and was burnt to ashes;
Now, although the room grows chilly,
I haven't the heart to poke poor Billy."

Harry Graham,
Ruthless Rhymes

Notice the flue liners. They are joined together with mortar as the chimney is laid up. Chimney brick, stone, or other kind of fire-resistant masonry is used for the chimney structure itself and to surround the flue liner. It is necessary to build the chimney through the attic and roof when it is located inside the house rather than against an outside wall; the necessary instructions for this will be included in a following chapter together with information on the correct height of a chimney.

At the top of the chimney is a *cap,* which may be a prefabricated cap or it may simply be molded in shape with mortar. But it should be bevelled to shed water away from the flue. The prefabricated caps usually extend past the edges of the brick for a couple inches or less and make an attractive top to the chimney.

18

Often a single chimney will contain more than one flue. Let's assume in the illustration that follows that flue ''A'' is the fireplace flue, and that flue ''B'' is the flue for the kitchen woodstove. They are built simultaneously as the chimney is being constructed. The two flues should never touch one another because differences in temperature in the two flues and their close proximity could cause up-drafts from one flue to enter the other, carrying smoke down into the room below.

To prevent water from entering around the chimney where it goes through the roof, *flashing* is laid into the chimney and lapped over the roof.

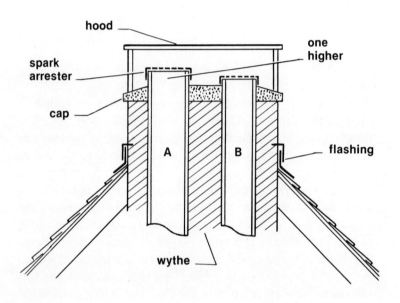

CRICKET'S ROLE

If a chimney does not go through the ridge of the roof but instead through the slope, it is desirable to have a *cricket* (also known as a *saddle*) built against the up-side of the chimney. This sheds water away from the chimney so it will not settle in the space in back and eventually work its way into the roof. But perhaps even more important, a cricket will shed snow and ice, which may be so severe in some areas as to rupture the flashing between the chimney and the up-slope of the roof. Such ruptures can have rather serious effects on the chimney itself.

19

"On many an abandoned pasture and often in a random growth of pine, sumac will thrive on the poorest soil imaginable. Some of the largest stems may be four inches or more at the base and the many crooked branches may rise fifteen feet or more. The tree has a not unattractive reddish brown 'blossom,' delectable for certain birds. But it is nevertheless a weed, and from the point of view of the woodlotter, it was created only to be cleared out of his woods and pastures, and perhaps more importantly, to supply the most useful kindling material imaginable.

"Devotees of the Cape Cod or soapstone firelighter or of a squirt of kerosene with which to start a blaze in fireplace or stove need not apply for sumac kindling. But those who find the lighter or kerosene system objectionable from the point of view of smell and bother may well keep an eye open and collect dead sumac."

Rockwell R. Stephens,
One Man's Forest

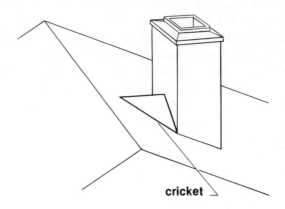

cricket

Occasionally it is desirable to have other features added to the top of the chimney. One such would be a *hood*, which is nothing more than a raised piece of stone, slate, or masonry in area the size of the chimney top, and raised four to six inches above the top of the flues. It keeps down-drafts from entering the flues and also keeps out rain and snow. Some masons, however, do not advocate hoods, feeling that the masonry within the chimney itself is adequate to absorb the moisture and that the hood prevents the efficient passage of smoke up the flues.

Still another feature is the *spark arrester,* a galvanized woven screen with a one-half-inch mesh. This is anchored to the top of the chimney where it fits over the flue, much like an inverted cake pan. It keeps live sparks from being blown about and setting fires, and keeps birds and other creatures from entering the flues. Some masons believe that it can interfere with proper drafts, especially if wet leaves or heavy deposits of snow stick to it.

If there is more than one flue in a chimney, they should be separated by a partition of mortar 3½ inches thick. This is called a *wythe,* and occasionally it extends above the chimney top several inches to prevent drafts in one flue from entering the other flues. If a hood is used as well, the wythe would extend up to the underside of the hood. A wythe and hood combination built perpendicular to the direction of prevailing winds, can be useful in shielding the flues from disturbing air currents.

20

Throughout this discussion we have mentioned the matter of drafts. A few more words about drafts are in order.

We must remember that a fire has to be fed air (oxygen) in ample supply not only to keep the embers burning but also to burn the gases and provide lifting power for the flaming gases and the smoke to rise up the chimney. In other words, we must have a strong up-draft or we will have only a smoke-filled room.

There is a constant down-draft in the flue even though smoke is rising out of the chimney. Why then doesn't the down-draft come out into the room, bringing with it smoke and fire wastes? The answer is that it will do just that unless it is turned around before it reaches the room. And that is precisely the reason for the smoke shelf in the chimney — to turn the down-draft around and send it back up with the rising smoke and gases from the fire below. The efficiency of the turn-around is also conditioned by the width of the throat, which we can regulate with the damper. And there is an important relationship between the size of the fireplace opening, its depth, and the size of the flue lining — all of which we'll discuss in detail in the next two chapters.

The illustration to the right shows the direction of drafts in the conventional fireplace and its flue.

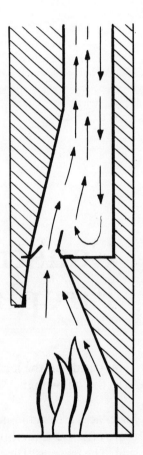

3 Constructing a Fireplace

Before you decide on the location of your fireplace, give some thought to the following:

1. Fireplaces with chimneys inside a house are generally more efficient than those whose chimneys are on the outside. The reasons? Heat is retained longer in the masonry when it is not cooled by an outside-exposed surface, and this makes for better drafts in the chimney. Also, the vapors from melted resins in some of the woods do not cool and adhere as easily to the flue in the form of creosote and tars.

2. Fireplaces should not be too close to windows and doors, or they will cause strong drafts in the room.

3. A fireplace should not be near a central heating thermostat. If it is, the heat from the fireplace may raise the temperature surrounding the thermostat to such an extent that the central heater will not go on, and other rooms in the house will remain cold.

4. Will one location be better than another for convenient storage of wood?

5. Consider the traffic patterns in the room and their relationship to the proposed location of the fireplace. Remember, too, that a fireplace will draw people toward it. Be sure you are willing to have people congregate in that particular area of the room.

6. The flue preferably should go straight up from the fire chamber, but it should never make more than a 45-degree turn. Be certain the flue and chimney can rise to their top heights without encountering any obstacles or support beams that cannot be relocated or cut through.

7. Will your furniture fit if you locate the fireplace in your favorite spot, or isn't that important?

8. Does it need to be near some other heat source, such as a kitchen stove or furnace, so that all flues may have a common chimney?

9. Finally, does the location you have chosen fit well with your decorating scheme? Remember, there will be many times when you will have no fire in the fireplace. Will it show off well when it stands by itself without embers aglow and without flames shooting upward?

"A chimney located entirely inside a building has better draft than an exterior chimney, because the masonry retains heat longer when protected from cold outside air."

USDA Farmers' Bulletin 1889

NEED A PERMIT?

Before starting to build the fireplace, you may need to obtain a building permit from your local town or city clerk or building inspector. The application will doubtless ask how, when and where in the house you plan to build it, the type of material you will use, and other questions. Of course, if you live in a very rural area, this may not be necessary.

Before applying for your permit, obtain a copy of the building code from your local clerk. The code sets forth some of the

23

things you must, and must not, do when building a fireplace. Read the code carefully. It may require you to have a foundation of a particular size, it may restrict you to the use of brick instead of fieldstone in order to preserve the atmosphere of the area in which you live, it may require you to have a chimney that reaches a definite number of feet above the roof line, and it may restrict you to using a particular mix of mortar.

In your application for a building permit you will be expected to abide by the building code provisions and not necessarily by our instructions. If you have strong reasons for taking exception to the code, be certain to get permission to change, asking the clerk or other official who issues the permit. We doubt that any local building code will require changes that would nullify the Rumford proportions we shall be using.

There are basically two types of fireplaces we shall discuss: those that are, with the exception of the chimney top, built completely within the house, and those that are built inside a wall of the house with their chimneys rising against the outside wall.

Of course, a fireplace may be built either when the house is being erected or sometime later after the house is completed. (If the latter, we would hope the builder anticipated the possibility of the fireplace and framed the house in such a way that the fireplace and chimney could be built without major structural changes to the building.)

We'll take all these variables into consideration in this and the following chapter, but we believe if we stick to one specific type of fireplace at the outset, then discuss the variables later, it will be more meaningful.

We shall follow closely the recommendations of Count Rumford and we will end up with a beautiful fireplace that does not smoke and that gives off a good amount of heat.

It will be easier to illustrate if we assume we are building with common brick. Although we could build the entire chimney before we complete the fireplace opening and hearth, we are completing everything as we move upward.

This, then, will be a simple, conventional fireplace. If you wish to make changes that will not affect the Rumford proportions and recommendations, you should have no problems doing so. By the time we have capped the chimney, you should be convinced that it is well to have a complete plan in mind for your fireplace before you start to build it.

'Nuff said. Let's get started with the foundation, also called the footing, of the fireplace and chimney structure.

Keep one thing in mind: The fireplace and chimney are the heaviest part of the house. They should rest on their own foundation, and the foundation must be solid and secure enough to support this great weight by itself without any assistance from the house foundation or footings. Furthermore, it should be big enough so the weight will be distributed over a large area of ground. In cold climates where the ground freezes, the foundation should reach below the frost line.

The size of the foundation depends on the size of the chimney, the height of the house, whether you have more than one fireplace and their flues in the same chimney, and whether you wish to provide for additional flues in the chimney for such things as a furnace, a kitchen stove, or an incinerator.

The relationship of these various factors will become apparent as we proceed in this and the next chapter. For the time being we shall assume only that you know how wide you wish the fireplace opening to be and that you plan only one flue in the chimney. We recommend that you read this chapter and the next before you decide on definite measurements for the foundation. By that time you will understand that the relationships between the various parts of the fireplace will determine the dimensions of the chimney, and the dimensions of the chimney will determine the area dimensions of the foundation.

The fireplace foundation should be of poured concrete:

1. At least eight inches thick if you have a one-story house, and at least twelve inches thick for a two-story house.

2. At least twelve inches thick if you plan to have two fireplaces on the same foundation (one upstairs and one downstairs, for example).

3. The foundation must extend at least six inches in all directions beyond the base of the chimney.

4. Furthermore, the foundation must rest on solid ground (and we do mean solid, not near drainage that could cause the weight of the chimney to shift); and if the ground freezes in winter, the foundation must rest on ground below the frost level.

A common mixture for concrete is one part cement, two and one-half parts sand and three parts gravel.

The following illustration shows the pit that has been dug for the foundation. Note that it is six inches wider all around

THE FOUNDATION

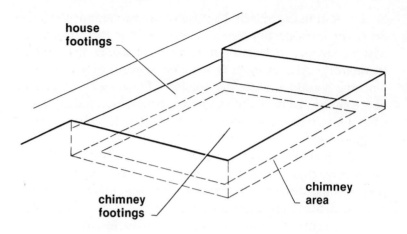

house footings

chimney footings

chimney area

than the base dimensions of the fireplace chimney. Note, also, that it is somewhat deeper than the house footings and that the pit and house footings touch.

When possible, the earth should be excavated so as to form the mold for the foundation. Sometimes wooden forms must be constructed, as when the foundation is built in loose gravel or sand.

The next illustration shows the placement of half-inch reinforcing rods. They should be placed a foot apart, and five inches above the pit floor. The fireplace foundation and the house foundation walls and footings are frequently poured at the same time.

It is possible, as the illustration shows, to block off the house foundation walls from becoming an integral part of the fireplace foundation. Some building codes may require that upright reinforcing rods for the inside chimney corners be set in, and perhaps even carried all the way to the top of the chimney. But it is a good idea at least to insert half-inch steel pins at each corner of the foundation slab (six inches into the slab and four inches above) to secure further the first layers of brick to the foundation.

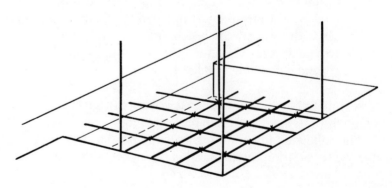

The foundation should be poured and carefully leveled. The concrete must cure properly. This is done by covering it with damp canvas or burlap for seven days, then leaving it exposed for another three days. At that time you are ready to lay bricks.

Some building codes require the chimney wall to be two-bricks thick, or eight inches. A two-brick-thick wall is recommended whenever the chimney is unusually tall or when a second fireplace is built above the first and uses the same chimney. If the ash pit were unusually large, two-brick-thick walls would be needed to support the weight of the chimney. We'll make our outer wall two bricks thick at least until we reach the throat of the fireplace.

We assume that you know how to lay bricks and what tools are needed for the job. If not, read one or two books that describe this skill, or get instruction from someone who knows. You will need a mortar trowel, a pointing trowel for smoothing joints, and a level.

Mortar for bricks other than firebricks should be cement mortar. Use one part portland cement, one part hydrated lime (or slack lime putty) and six parts clean sand — all parts by volume. Firebricks are made from fire clay, and are manufactured to withstand high temperatures. The standard size is $9 \times 4\frac{1}{2} \times 2\frac{1}{2}$. The mortar used with firebrick is fire clay mixed with water to the consistency of thick cream. Used firebricks can be ground to provide fire clay.

The concrete foundation should be brushed clean before any bricks are laid, to insure a good bond to the foundation. Mark off where bricks will be laid around the chimney base, two bricks wide on the back and one brick wide on the ends and on the front side. Also mark off where you will build two interior walls all the way up to the hearth to support the fire chamber and covings. These interior walls should be directly under

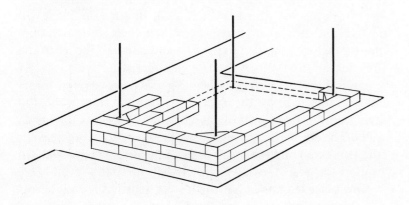

"Brickwork around chimney flues and fireplaces should be laid with cement mortar; it is more resistant to the action of heat and flue gases than lime mortar.

"A good mortar to use in setting flue linings and all chimney masonry, except firebrick, consists of one part portland cement, one part hydrated lime (or slaked-lime putty), and six parts clean sand, measured by volume.

"Firebrick should be laid with fire clay."

USDA Farmers' Bulletin 1889

where the covings will be laid, and they will be only one brick wide. If you want to add upright steel reinforcements, or your building code calls for them, set them into the inside corners of the chimney as you build upward and conceal them behind corner pieces which you will need to cut out of bricks.

Now lay up several courses of bricks, remembering that each successive course overlaps the one below by half the length of a brick.

By the time you have laid the first few rows, you must have reached a decision on where the door to the ash pit will be — inside or outside the house. Set its frame into the masonry as you continue laying other courses of brick. Doors for ash pits are standard stock items from masonry supply houses as are metal ash dumps.

Check frequently with your level to be certain the masonry is plumb and level. Be conscientious about checking this all the way to the top of the chimney.

"Everybody knows I can't lay bricks."

Al Smith

THE HEARTH

Continue laying up brick to the walls already formed, adding additional steel reinforcing rods for the corners, until you reach the height where you will build the base of the front and back hearths, known as the *subhearth*.

How will you know when you have reached that point? In this example the floor level of the fire chamber will be at the same level as the finished floor of the house. The floor of the fire chamber (back hearth) is made of firebricks. These firebricks are laid flat and, as we have said, are 2½ inches thick.

But now we must figure out how thick the subhearth will be. It should never be less than four inches, and can be thicker, of course, to compensate for bringing the subhearth to the proper level from the last course of brick laid. In our example it will be five and one-quarter inches. When these five and one-quarter inches are added to the two and one-half inches of the firebrick on the floor of the fire chamber, we have a total of seven and three-quarters inches. So exactly seven and three-quarters inches below the level of the finished floor we'll stop laying up the front wall of the chimney as well as the inside wall of the double back wall, for we are going to use these walls (the front wall and the inside wall of the double back wall) to support the hearth. Bring all other walls up to this level.

Now place lengths of half-inch steel reinforcing rods across the chimney opening from the front wall to the inside wall of the double back wall. Make these about three to three and one-half inches on center, and place common bricks, flat side down and closely together, over the rods. At a point central and to the rear of the fire chamber, omit one brick and instead insert a box or other form so that when concrete is poured and the remainder of the hearth is constructed, a hole will be molded to provide for the ash pit opening. You may wish to move the reinforcing rods around a bit so they will not be directly under the box that molds the hole, but that really will not be necessary because the ashes will easily drop through without being caught by the rods. Now pour a half-inch of concrete over the bricks, level it, and let is set until it is firm to the touch.

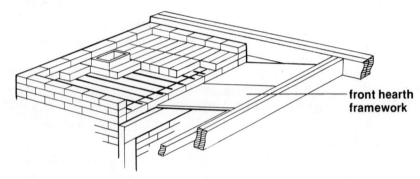

front hearth framework

The front hearth will extend at least twenty inches in front of the fireplace opening and at least six inches on each side of it. This will require that a temporary wood framework (as in the illustration) be built in front of the chimney to support it. The rear base of the front hearth will be the same height as the last layer of bricks on the front chimney wall, but the base may have a slight upward slant toward the front.

Now set in reinforcing rods, these about eight inches on center and running both front-to-back and side-to-side over the area of the front and back hearths. The front-to-back rods should lie flat on the concrete you poured over the brick on the back hearth area, and they should extend out to the front end of the front hearth; the cross rods will rest on these. Now pour a layer of concrete two inches thick over the back hearth and extend it right out over the framework and reinforcing rods of the front hearth, bringing it up level with the concrete on the back hearth.

Let the concrete harden overnight. Then the temporary framework may be removed, leaving a subhearth that is cantilevered from the chimney wall, and which does not carry any weight of the house. Remember? The fireplace must "float."

"The way to keep wet wood burning is to split it up into small sticks."

Larry Gay,
The Complete Book of Heating with Wood

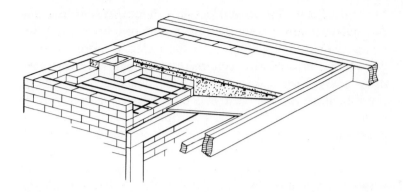

Now a layer of firebrick should be laid flat in the back hearth right up to the front of the fireplace opening. Regular brick, terra-cotta tile or other decorative and fire-resistant material may be used to finish the front hearth, making it level with the finished floor and the back hearth.

In summary, then, here is how we figured the thickness of the back hearth and subhearth to know how many inches below the finished floor of the house we needed to stop laying up courses of brick in the chimney wall and start building the hearth area:

Reinforcing rods used as base of subhearth . . . . . ½ inch
Common brick used as floor of subhearth . . . 2¼ inches
Layer of concrete to secure the bricks . . . . ½ inch
Layer of concrete over entire hearth . . . . 2 inches
Firebrick mortared to layer of concrete . . . . . 2½ inches
TOTAL . . . . 7 ¾ inches

Be sure to use fire clay cement whenever laying firebricks. You may prefer to lay the finish layer on the front hearth after the chimney is completed to avoid possible nicks and scratches during construction.

Earlier we said that the subhearth should be at least four inches thick, which is what some building codes require. Yet we made ours seven and three-quarters inches thick. Why?

Fire chiefs have complained to us that too often the hearths are responsible for house fires because they are not thick enough. Even though the material is fire-resistant, long, continuous fires in fireplaces can cause fire-resistant material to weaken so that it will crumble and fall apart. Long, continuous fires may also ignite floor joists and framing close to fireplaces.

One of the wildest stories we heard was about a beautifully constructed fireplace except that the hearth was simply two layers of common brick laid on the subflooring of the house.

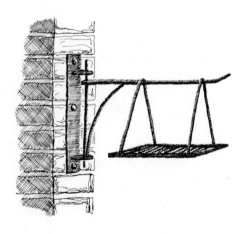

30

The fire quickly heated through the brick, then scorched and weakened the subflooring until the hearth dropped, setting the house on fire.

Shortcuts that risk fires also risk lives. If you have any questions concerning fire safety, check with a fire chief.

Before we go further, we should consider some of Count Rumford's admonitions and principles insofar as they concern the fire chamber, the fireback, the throat, and the covings, for they are where we shall be working next.

As you face the hearth, try to imagine where you would like to locate the fireback. It must be a minimum of eight inches inside the rear wall of the chimney, and possibly even more if your building code so directs. Measure the distance from the front of the fireback to the fireplace opening. Let's assume it is eighteen inches. Then, according to Count Rumford, the width of the fireback must also be eighteen inches. The width of the fireback and its distance from the fireplace opening must always be the same to achieve maximum draft and heat.

Next, how wide should the fireplace opening be? Rumford suggested that it be three times the depth of the fire chamber, that being the same as three times the width of the fireback, or, in our example, fifty-four inches. And the height of the fireplace opening should be the same as its width.

Experience has shown that the dimensions for width and height of the fireplace opening may be less than three times the width of the fireback, but they should be at least twice that width. Any measurement between two and three times will not impede combustion. Rumford's reason for suggesting three times was to arrive at an angle of the covings that would radiate the maximum amount of heat into the room, and three times makes a better angle for this purpose than two does. If the purpose of a fireplace is to expose the flames and get the greatest amount of heat possible into the room the three-times formula for height and width will achieve that purpose better than a two-times formula.

When you have decided how wide you want the fireback to be, use that same dimension to mark on the floor of the back hearth its distance from the fireplace opening. You can also center and mark on the back hearth the width of the fireplace opening. Next it is simple to connect the lines from the ends of the fireback to the ends of the fire chamber opening, and there

SOME RUMFORD PRINCIPLES

"Since it would be a miracle if smoke should not rise in a chimney (as water runs down hill), we only have to find out and remove these hindrances which prevent smoke from following its natural tendency to rise."

Count Rumford

you have the covings all marked out.* You may double-check this with the help of the accompanying illustration.

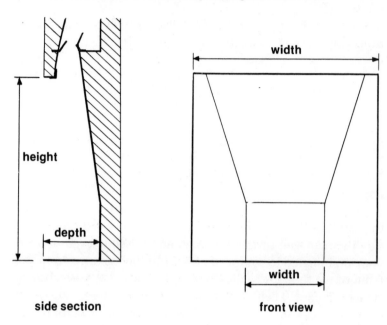

side section

front view

Rumford also discovered that if the fireback is bent forward, more heat is radiated into the room. Equally important, the smoke is helped to go up the chimney. Nevertheless, the first twelve inches or so of the fireback should be laid vertically, and at that point the fireback should be slanted. So now we'll lay up the fireback, with firebrick laid flat, to the level where we shall put an angle in the fireback. Note that the slope should be just that, an abrupt slant and not a curve. Otherwise smoke will almost certainly enter the room instead of passing up the chimney.

How much of a slant is required for the slope of the fireback?

To answer that question, you must find the precise center of the back hearth, the point where a line down the center of its width crosses the center line of its length.

Now establish a point that is exactly above this point and at a height that is eight inches greater than the top of the fireplace opening. Construction of a simple wooden framing will help to establish this point. This is the precise center of what will be the throat of the chimney. The throat, according to Rumford, must always be at least three and never more than four inches wide, regardless of the size of the fireplace. Furthermore, the throat must be the same length as the width of the fireplace opening.

* In actual building practice you would have your dimensions figured out before starting to build the chimney; otherwise, you would not know where to erect the foundation supports for the covings and fire chamber which rest on the foundation slab of the chimney.

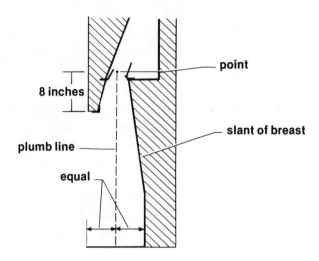

8 inches

plumb line

equal

point

slant of breast

Now establish the position of the two back corners of the throat, and extend lines from them to the respective front ends of the top layer of brick in the vertical fireback, where the slope begins. These lines will give you the proper slant of the sloped section of the fireback.

Similarly, establish the two front corners of the throat, and lines from them to the respective ends of the lintel will give you, when you are constructing in that section, the right slant for the breast.

The covings and the fireback will be of firebrick laid flat to increase the thickness of their walls. Build the covings one course ahead of the fireback. Because the covings butt against the fireback, the bricks of the covings will have to be cut to fit properly. One way to do this is to put the bricks in place dry, then mark the proper cutting angle on them with a straightedge.

The fireback is made just a little longer at each end than what you measured. This permits the fireback to rest against the rear edges of the covings. Your local building code may require that you fill the space between the firebricks and the chimney walls with mortar. It is a good place to get rid of scrap masonry and mortar anyway.

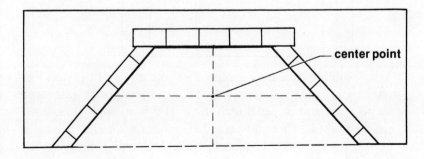

center point

In the front, the covings will butt against the jambs of the fireplace opening. The jambs may be laid along with the covings but are made of common bricks. If facing is planned for the jambs, it will be necessary to insert *mortar ties* between every other course of bricks. Mortar ties are narrow strips of metal inserted part way into concrete when it hardens or into joints of masonry at frequent intervals. When facing is later installed over the masonry, the exposed ends may be bent and mortared into the joints of the facing to secure the facing better to its masonry back.

Jambs are usually at least twelve inches wide if a wooden mantel is used and sixteen inches wide if they are going to be exposed with ornamental brick or one of the various kinds of decorative tiles.

Beginning the slope of the fireback requires that only the first layer of brick be tipped by making a wedge-shaped joint with mortar. Then successive courses are laid flat on the one below.

Continue building upward with brick, and don't forget to put in additional reinforcing rods, if you are using them, for the inside corners of the chimney.

Check at every layer to be sure that everything is level and plumb until you have reached the point that will be the top of the fireplace opening. It's time to lay in the lintel.

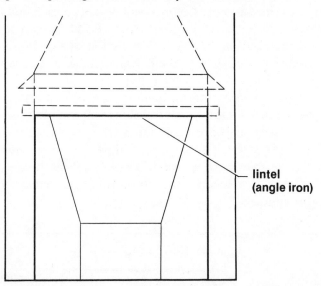

lintel
(angle iron)

THE LINTEL

Your building code may specify the dimensions of the steel lintel. If not, it may be flat, in which case it should be at least three inches wide and one-half inch thick. If it is an angle iron, both sides should be three and one-half inches wide and at least a quarter-inch thick. The lintel should extend four or more inches into each jamb and be securely set in with mortar.

If a stone slab is used for the lintel, it must be thick enough and strong enough to support the masonry above it, and must be well seated into the jambs.

Again, the brickwork should be continued upward until you reach the level of the throat. The brick above the lintel forms the breast. Remember to use firebrick wherever brick will come in contact with the flames. Taper the inside of the breast to come within one and one-half to two inches of the midpoint of the throat. Cut brick and mortar should be used to make the interior side of this slope smooth to prevent soot and smoke build-up.

Here we shall stop brick-laying to install the damper.

THE DAMPER

Several different kinds of dampers are available at masonry supply houses.

The damper you install must be as long as the length of the fireplace opening. Most dampers have flanges that allow them to be seated directly on the brick you have laid up to the level of the throat. It will be quite easy to seat this and to mortar it in place. The damper should be positioned so the hinged edge of its blade is just at the forward edge of the smoke shelf.

The blade of the damper should be free to open fully. Lay up a few courses of firebrick around it to be certain nothing will prevent this.

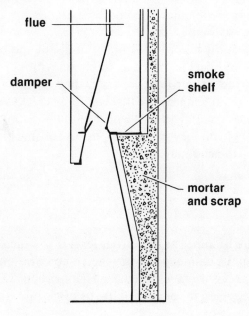

THE SMOKE SHELF

When you tilted the fireback toward the throat, you created a space between the fireback and the inside back wall of the chimney. This space should be filled with mortar, or scrap and mortar. At the top of the slope, the mortar should be leveled off to become the smoke shelf, which should span the entire length of the throat. This smoke shelf will turn the down-drafts around and direct them back up the chimney, and it is one of Count Rumford's most important contributions to the efficiency of the fireplace.

THE FLUE

Earlier we said that the dimensions of the chimney depended on a number of factors. One of these was the size of the flue. So the question now is: "What size flue do I need?"

Let's remember that we are going to use flue liners, those made of vitrified fire clay at least five-eighths of an inch thick.

The cross-section opening of a flue liner should be one-tenth the opening of the fireplace chamber. Thus if the fireplace is fifty-four by fifty-four inches, the area of the fireplace opening is 2,916 square inches. Therefore, you should buy a liner that has an area of approximately 292 inches. A flue liner with an inside dimension of seventeen by seventeen inches would give an area of 289 square inches, which would be about right.

Flue liners come in rectangular and round shapes. There are honest debates as to which is more efficient. Most masons prefer square or rectangular flue liners.

But why use them?

They lessen the hazards of fire because soot and creosote do not adhere to liners as much as to chimney brick. And since they are made of vitrified fire clay, they do not respond to sharp changes in temperature that can cause cracks in masonry. Exposed mortar and bricks will eventually succumb to the erosion of hot chimney gases. Too, the use of flue liners greatly strengthens the chimney.

CONTINUING THE CHIMNEY

Because the fireplace at the throat level is so much wider and longer than the chimney will be when it contains only the flue liner, it is necessary now to reduce its dimensions. This will require the stepping in, or corbelling, of brick courses.

The wall of the chimney outside the house will not be stepped in. It will continue straight up all the way from the foundation to the very top. But the sides (ends) and the front wall will be stepped in. The chamber above the damper that results from the corbelling of bricks is the smoke chamber.

When stepping in, one-inch overlapping with each course of brick is sufficient. Continue laying up brick (use firebrick where it comes in contact with smoke and gases) until the inside of the chimney is just large enough in area for a flue liner to be mortared in. Be certain that the masonry is smooth on the inside so there will be no jagged edges for soot and creosote to collect. This may require smoothing with mortar or chimney plaster unless you are adept at cutting and fitting pieces of brick.

When you have reached the proper height, make a slight ledge in the chimney on which to rest the liner. The opening of the flue liner should be centered over the center of the throat, or perhaps a slight bit off the front-to-back center toward the back wall of the chimney.

If you are using steel reinforcing rods, they should be set in at each outside corner of the flue liners. Furthermore, liners should be set in before the brick work is laid around them. Slipping them in afterward causes mortar to ooze out into the joints, thus causing jagged edges to catch and hold soot.

Since mortar at the joints of flue liners may become loose eventually, to insure against fire hazards be certain that no joints are directly opposite brick joints. The accompanying illustration indicates how the joints of liners and bricks should be offset.

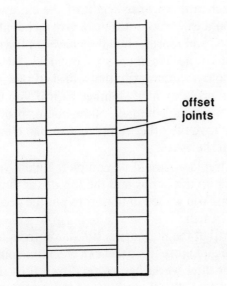

offset joints

"The best precaution against chimney fires is to burn only dry wood."

Larry Gay,
*The Complete Book of
Heating with Wood*

Guard against clogging the smoke shelf, the damper, and the throat with pieces of masonry and mortar that fall down as you work. If you will fill a bag with sawdust or straw and fit it tightly inside the flue liner just below where you are working, scraps of masonry and mortar that fall will be caught by it, and you can pull the bag up as you proceed and remove this waste.

Some local codes specify that outside chimneys be secured to the house, usually at roof level. This is to prevent toppling in the event of severe storms or earthquakes. If the code does not specify just how this should be done, here is a way: A one and one-half inch iron strap may be wrapped around the flue liner and the reinforcing rods, twisted so that it passes flat through a mortar joint and its ends fastened to the ceiling joists or to the roof plate of the house. The next chapter will tell how to cut into the roof to locate the ceiling joists and roof plate.

How high should the chimney be? You are likely to find the answer in your building code. Otherwise a good rule to follow is to build it three feet above the roof if you have a flat roof, and two feet above the roof ridge or above any elevation that is within ten feet of the chimney (for instance a dormer window).

At the point where the chimney passes through the roof, flashing must be installed to prevent rain from leaking down into the house between the roof and chimney. There is a section on flashing in the next chapter. Wait until you have read it before concerning yourself with this important matter.

Continue laying up flue liners and the chimney walls until you have reached the proper height of the chimney. The last flue liner should extend about four or five inches above the top layer of bricks, and mortar should be bevelled from two inches below the top of the flue liner to the outside of the top course of brick to mold a chimney cap that will shed rain. Or you may wish to buy a prefabricated chimney cap. If you plan to have two flues in the same chimney, allow one to project three or four inches above the other to prevent smoke from one being drafted down the other.

Now the fireplace should be complete unless you have not yet put facing on the jambs and the top of the fireplace opening, or perhaps you waited until now to put the decorative layer on the front hearth.

Remember that the masonry is still damp from the wet mortar. Sudden heat before it is dried can crack the joints. It is best to wait two or three weeks before building a fire, and then only a small one at first. But if you wish to test your completed fireplace to see how well it works, open the damper and light several newspaper pages in the hearth and watch the smoke go up the chimney.

Some masons recommend a small fire of loose material that will make a dark smoke. Then they cover the chimney top with a damp blanket and check to see if smoke oozes out of the masonry anywhere. If it does, check to see how the leak can be shut tight to prevent fire hazards. It's better still to check your work carefully and minutely as you build so you will be certain there are no leaks.

The plan we have followed is for a conventional fireplace, a fairly simple one to demonstrate the basic steps. There are, of course, occasions for more complicated ones such as fireplaces built entirely within the house, chimneys with several flues, one fireplace above the other, upstairs and downstairs, foundations that are built right on the foundation walls of the house, and fireplaces built long after the house has been built. All these require different plans. However, if you know how to build a conventional fireplace, these others represent only variations on the conventional type.

At the start of this book, we said we were going to follow the proportions recommended by Count Rumford. Few people have spent as much time studying fireplaces and working out the scientific principles as he did.

Yet there are many fireplaces that do not follow his principles and that are efficient and successful. As a result, it is not uncommon to find recommended sizes for fireplace openings that do not match those recommended by him. Even the U.S. government puts out a pamphlet which lists non-Rumford sizes.

We do not intend to downgrade these other sizes. But we think their success is perhaps more dependent on luck than on scientific principles. So, if you choose one of these other sizes, we wish you luck. And if later you have smoke problems, we have another chapter that may interest you: Chapter 9 on How to Stop a Fireplace from Smoking.

"The most tangible of all mysteries — fire."

Leigh Hunt

4 Constructing a Fireplace – Details

In Chapter 3, in order to simplify as much as possible a basic understanding of fireplace construction, we omitted details which we felt might get in the way of our discussion. These pertained not only to other types of fireplaces but also to specifics such as how to cut through the wall of a house, more elaborate chimneys, and how to apply flashing. In this chapter we will discuss some of these.

We strongly advise, even though you are planning just a simple, conventional fireplace with a chimney that runs up the outside wall of your house, that you read this chapter before attempting to build or oversee the building of your fireplace.

Your building code may require the chimney to be anchored to the foundation slab with strong steel pins — probably one inside each corner of the chimney. These pins — about ten inches long and of ½-inch thick steel — aren't required if you use the reinforcing rods throughout the chimney as we have recommended. We feel that, even though the code does not require them, the advantages of having pins far outweigh the small investment cost.

Using the House Walls as Foundation for the Fireplace

While we do not advocate it because we believe a fireplace structure should be completely independent of the building, some building codes do permit fireplace chimneys to rest on the foundation walls of the house. To support this extra weight, the house foundation walls should be of solid masonry at least twelve inches thick; and to provide adequate width for the chimney, it will be necessary to corbel layers of brick outward from the sides of the wall. The offset should be no greater than a total of 6 inches from the face of the foundation wall, and each course of brick should project no more than 1 inch from the previous course.

Foundation for a Fireplace Chimney Entirely Within the House

The foundation slab for a fireplace chimney that is entirely within the building is no more complicated than one laid outside the house except that it facilitates matters if it can be poured at the same time the basement floor is poured. Otherwise it will be necessary to break up a section of the basement floor to excavate and pour the foundation. The foundation should be measured for size exactly as if the slab were being poured outside. Think of it as being completely independent of the basement since it does not bond to the basement floor. Concrete can be poured up to, and troweled even with, the level of the basement floor.

A Second-floor Fireplace Over the One Below

If you plan a second-floor fireplace over the one downstairs, keep these points in mind:

- The second-floor fireplace is usually smaller than the one below for two reasons. First, there should be as little weight as possible in the upper heights of the chimney. Second, the length of the flue for the upstairs fireplace will be shorter than for the one below, and short flues are more efficient if the fireplaces are small.
- Assuming that flues from each of the fireplaces will be using a common chimney, it may require that one or both

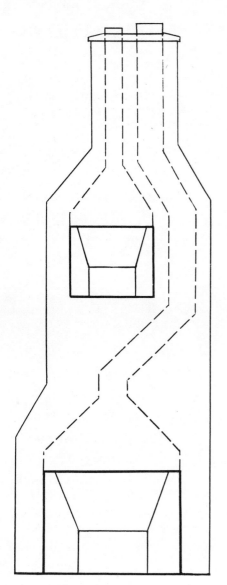

be angled somewhat until they can be fitted side by side in the chimney for a straight run upward. When flues are angled, the slant should never be more than 45 degrees, and it is much better to keep it to no more than 30 degrees. Angling the flue requires corbelling, and bricks should be offset no more than one inch per successive course.

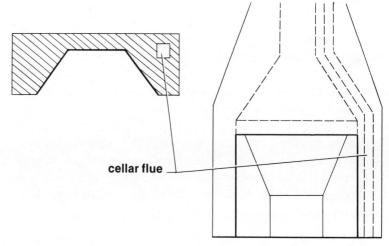

cellar flue

It is sometimes easier to build an upstairs fireplace when the chimney is entirely within the house; there is more choice in positioning the fireplace in the room than there is when an outside chimney practically dictates that the fireplace opening be almost exactly over the one below.

Providing the chimney is centered properly, it may have several fireplaces built into it, as so often happened in old colonial homes. Then, of course, the foundation becomes a massive one to accommodate all the fireplaces, which are not necessarily one above the other. When we have outside chimneys, we try to keep them as simple as possible for appearance's sake. Most modern homes have but one fireplace.

ADDING A FIREPLACE

This section pertains to homes that were not originally planned with fireplaces.

It is best to locate the fireplace along the outside wall so the chimney will be outside. Adjusting the house framing will be less complicated, and there will be less of a mess inside the house during construction. And, perhaps most important, it will be much easier to build the foundation if it is outside.

Lay out the dimensions of the foundation slab as before; then excavate for it, going to a depth at least equal to that of the house footings and also below the frost level in cold climate areas. Reinforce the slab as described in the previous chapter and pour concrete right up to the house foundation wall, which should have been washed beforehand.

The side of the house should be marked off indicating where the fireplace will be; then the wall should be opened carefully to expose beams and any electrical, water, or other conduits that will have to be rerouted. Remove the plaster or wallboard on the inside. NO STUDS SHOULD BE CUT UNTIL THE WALL IS FIRST SUPPORTED.

Supporting the wall requires a temporary bracing while the fireplace opening is framed in. Place a heavy plank 2" × 8", and a few feet longer than the fireplace front to be placed over the flooring, along the wall where the opening will be cut out. Another plank the same size will have to be placed parallel and directly over it and on the ceiling;* this plank should be supported by several 2"×6" planks just slightly (a half-inch or so) longer than the distance between the two 2"×8" planks, or better still, supported by floor jacks. The supports for the ceiling plank must be snug, for they will have to carry the weight carried by the wall studs which are to be cut.

Now the wall studs may be cut where the fireplace opening into the room will be. The height of the cut should provide for a double 2"×6" plate on edge to support the cut studs, and the underside of the 2"×6" double plate should be at least 2 inches

"Gas-fired house heaters and built-in unit heaters can be connected to metal flues instead of to a masonry chimney. The flues should be made of corrosion-resistant metal not lighter than 20 gage and should be properly insulated with asbestos or other fire-proof material that complies with the recommendations of Underwriters' Laboratories, Inc. The flues must extend through the roof."

USDA Farmers' Bulletin 1889

This upstairs den fireplace fits well into small rooms. This is a gas-fired fireplace by Majestic.

* Check to be certain that the ceiling joists do not run in opposite directions to the floor joists. If they do, it will be necessary first to run planks in a counter direction to support the 2" × 8" ceiling plank and thus to prevent its puncturing the ceiling.

above the throat of the fireplace. The ends of the double 2″ × 6″ plate should be supported by double studding which rests on the sill plate. Save the insulation and vapor barrier you remove and use it again wherever necessary to insulate around the entrance of the chimney into the house.

The next step is to open the floor where the front hearth will be located. This involves cutting the floor joists; so they must first be **permanently** supported underneath just back of where they will be cut. This is best done by resting a 6″ × 6″ girder or heavy-duty permanent jacks on reinforced concrete footings. Now the floor joists and floor may be cut out to provide room for the hearth. The joists should be finished off by butting and nailing a double plate of 2″ × 8″ the length of the front hearth opening. Strap-hangers may be used to hold the double plate of 2″ × 8″'s to the first un-cut floor joists bordering the opening on each side.

Now form a subhearth and lay up the fire chamber and chimney as described earlier.

An option that does not require cutting the floor joists would be to cantilever a raised hearth.

Wherever the masonry enters the walls, weatherproof paper should line the opening, and the brick should be laid snug against it. Then it should be caulked on the outside with mastic caulking. At the top of the fire chamber, metal flashing should be set into the masonry in a mortared joint and run the length of the fire chamber and jambs, the top of the flashing being nailed to the outer wood sheathing. Weatherproof paper should be put in behind all masonry that goes against woodwork — all the way to the roof line.

Some masons put a strip of asbestos next to the bricks that butt against woodwork as an additional precaution against fire hazards.

Wherever the chimney is corbelled, flashing should be used to prevent moisture from entering the house.

Where the chimney rises against the house, exterior siding such as shingles and clapboards should be cut away before the weatherproof paper is applied. This permits the chimney to be as close as possible to the exterior sheathing.

At the roof line, bare the roof down to the roof boards in an area about a foot wider than the chimney all around. Then everything should be cut away from the roof where the chimney enters to leave an opening two inches larger than the chimney will be. This will involve cutting out some of the rough roofing under the overhang and cutting the ends of the roof rafters back to the plate.

"When we build, let us think that we build for ever."

John Ruskin,
The Seven Lamps of Architecture

A 1½-inch metal band should be used to tie the chimney to the roof plate, ceiling joists, or roof rafters as we have discussed before. Then flashing should be properly set into running joints of masonry, cemented, and caulked and overlapped over to the roof. Flashing should be stuck to the roof with mastic, and all joints that do not overlap should be soldered.

Adding a Fireplace with an Inside Chimney

This should present no special problems beyond what we have already discussed regarding indoor fireplaces and chimneys. This fireplace should be located to have as easy as possible access through the floors above and through the roof without cutting through load-bearing beams. Where this becomes necessary, however, temporary supports will be required while permanent bracing is built. All woodwork should be kept two inches away from the outside of the chimney to maintain the independence of the chimney from the building. This means that any bracing that is necessary must not, repeat not, rest on the chimney. *Firestops* at floor levels may be fastened against the chimney to lessen the chances that any house fires would spread up the two-inch opening. Sheets of stiff asbestos or boards covered with metal are commonly used as firestops. They rest snugly against the chimney and are fastened in place to the framework surrounding the chimney.

If the ridge and rafters have to be cut, they should first be given new permanent supports of double $2'' \times 6''$'s positioned on a double $2'' \times 6''$ plank crossways of the ceiling joists. These supports should themselves support a double $2'' \times 6''$ header against the shortened rafters.

The following shows a support framing for an interior chimney going through a roof.

The exterior part of the chimney is built like any other chimney, and the flashing is handled as described later in this chapter.

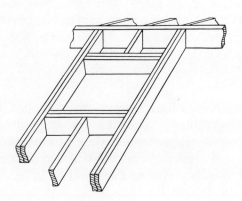

THE CHIMNEY

Several Flues in a Single Chimney

As we have said, each fire source should have its own flue, and that is the reason some chimneys have more than one flue — the flues from two, three, or more fire sources may use the same chimney. In a case of two flues, they may be side by side,* but the joints of the liners should be staggered to prevent any rupture in one leaking smoke, drafts, or flames into the other. It is wise to stagger them at least seven inches.

If there are three or more flues in the same chimney, building codes usually require any group of two to be separated from the third or other flues by at least 3½ inches of masonry called a wythe. The wythe should be extended a few inches above the chimney cap and planned so that it is perpendicular to the prevailing wind currents. This lessens down-drafts.

Thickness of Chimney Walls

Some building codes require the chimney walls to be widened to at least 8 inches in thickness where they are exposed above the roof. This is to prevent a greater resistance to wind hazards. Circumstances requiring this enlargement are most common in those situations where no flue liners have been used (we are totally against chimneys without flue liners). In such instances the small chimney should be corbelled outward to an eight-inch wall thickness, starting early enough so the full width of the chimney is achieved at least six inches before the chimney penetrates the roof on the downside.

There are several conventions that have become standard concerning chimneys without flue liners. If for some reason you do not plan to have them, and if your building code does not specify how the chimney should be built, be guided by the following:

- Make the walls of the chimney at least eight inches thick if of brick. If the inner course is made of firebrick, that gives much more added safety. The same thickness is recommended for chimneys of non-reinforced concrete. If reinforced, a thickness of six inches should be adequate. Reinforcing rods should be laced both horizontally and vertically.

When stone is used for chimneys, there is added danger that the walls may become loose and cracked. Twelve-inch walls and flue liners are recommended when stone is used.

If hollow concrete blocks are used instead of brick, it is recommended that they also be lined and be at least six inches thick.

* While it is true that some codes allow two flues to be side by side, we strongly recommend 3½ inches of masonry to separate them.

46

When there is more than one flue in an unlined chimney, a wythe at least eight inches thick should separate the flues.

Many masons say that no woodwork should be in contact with the chimney, and that a two-inch space should be left between the walls of the chimney and wooden beams, joists, furring, and studding. If, however, the chimney walls are of solid masonry at least 8 inches thick, it is permissible for the framing to come to within a half-inch of the chimney walls. (Some building codes may require different distances.) An exception is made for wood flooring, which may be laid to ¾ inch of the masonry. The space between the wooden framing and the chimney walls may be filled with loose materials that are incombustible and non-metallic, such as cinders and asbestos.

If chimney walls are to be enclosed behind wood, the masonry should be given a coat of plaster first. Common plaster may be applied directly to masonry, but if plaster is applied to exposed masonry walls, cracks may show up if the chimney should settle, even though the plaster is supported by metal lath.

If combustible baseboards are to be installed against plaster that is applied directly to the fireplace wall, there should be a layer of asbestos behind them.

THE CRICKET

Also called a saddle, the cricket is frequently built against the chimney after it emerges through the roof; it is located on the up-side of the chimney. Its purpose is to deflect rain and snow and to prevent the formation of ice, which could cause pressure against the chimney, resulting in cracks for the weather to penetrate the roof.

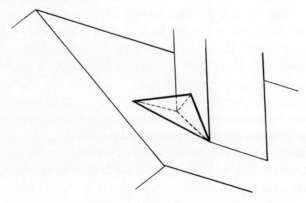

FLASHING

Flashing should keep rain and dampness from entering the house around the brickwork where the chimney passes through the roof and also along the corbelling of an outside chimney that is partially inside the walls of the house.

Flashing should be of non-corrosive metal (the type that will not rust or react to smoke or gases) such as lead, copper, and zinc. These are better than either tinned or galvanized sheet steel, which require painting from time to time. Do not use aluminum which deteriorates if creosote or tar products come in contact with it.

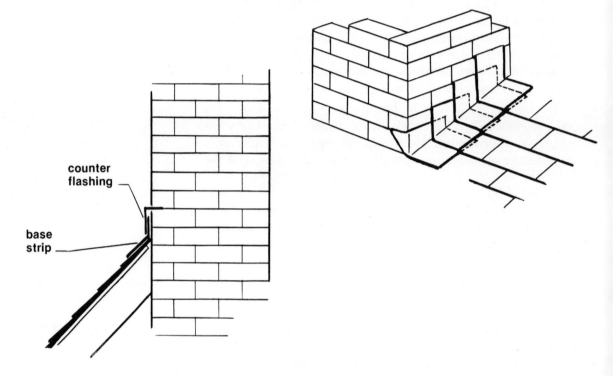

counter flashing

base strip

Where chimneys go through the roof, strips of metal are fitted on the roof covering and bent up against the chimney. These strips are called "base strips." Where they lie against roof coverings, they should be sealed in place with mastic. Another layer of flashing, known as "counter flashing" or "cap flashing," should be set into the joints of the masonry, then bent completely over the base strips that are against the chimney. Each strip of flashing should overlap the one below it as you proceed up the slant of the roof; then the joints where the cap overlaps the base strip should be soldered.

A cricket, too, must be flashed.

The figures above illustrate how flashing is applied to these various types of structures.

48

Soapstone is another good radiating material for lining the fire-back and covings. It should be at least four inches thick. Steel linings are also used providing they are at least ¼-inch thick. But these linings should be backed up by brick to give a wall at least an eight-inch total thickness.

Occasionally it is felt that there should be some ventilation in the ash pit. This would allow any unburned gases and any smoke from live coals dumped into the pit to escape. Masonry supply houses have louvres that fit in the space of a brick for this purpose, and when used, these louvres should, of course, fit into the outside wall of the chimney.

It is possible to find a number of prefabricated fireplace units on the market designed to simplify the construction of a fireplace. Sometimes they do, and sometimes they do not. Examples are prefabricated throats with built-in lintels; fire chambers; and, as we know, dampers. *Before* you purchase any of these, be certain they are the right size and shape. Be sure they will not destroy the Rumford proportions, which are so very important for having a successful fireplace. Ask someone who has built with them what his experience has been. Was it successful? Did the fireplace draw well? Did it smoke?

Masons have told us of unhappy homeowners who had to have the masonry torn apart in their fireplaces to pull out some of the metal units that had corroded and rusted. And there are stories of others who have been advised to install dampers that were not long enough. Get your guidance from experienced masons with a reputation for building good honest fireplaces.

Masonry supply houses stock mesh screens made for chimney tops. Be sure to get the proper equipment for anchoring them to the chimney. The screen should be made of metal that will withstand the erosive effects of gas and smoke. If you use a screen, check it frequently to be sure that wet leaves do not accumulate on top and that pieces of unburned paper from the fire do not clog it underneath.

There are several different types of spark arresters commonly stocked by masonry supply houses. They are also used to prevent birds from using the chimneys as homes and nesting places.

"Hard green wood just cut, though I used but little of that, answered my purpose better than any other. I sometimes left a good fire when I went to take a walk in a winter afternoon; and when I returned, three or four hours afterward, it would be still alive and glowing. My house was not empty though I was gone. It was as if I had left a cheerful housekeeper behind. It was I and Fire that lived there; and commonly my housekeeper proved trustworthy."

Henry D. Thoreau,
Walden

The Weed House, built around 1838 on the Shelburne (Vt.) Museum property where it still stands, features this huge fireplace, built for cooking as well as heating.

50

5 Cost of a Fireplace

There are many ways to save money while building a fireplace — ways to save money and still be able to build a fireplace that is safe and a pleasure to own.

One way is to do the work yourself. The cost of labor can be 75 percent or more of the total cost of the fireplace. Fireplaces are not too difficult for homeowners to build provided they have some knack at performing do-it-yourself projects and have plenty of time. This is not something that should be rushed, for it has to be done right the first time. To demolish a poor fireplace and build another, or to tear apart a section to be rebuilt, is costly and difficult.

But even if you decide to have the fireplace built by a mason, there are ways to save money.

First you should have a detailed plan for the fireplace — where it will be located, what kind of masonry will be used and how much, whether or not you plan to use reinforcing rods, how elaborate you want the mantel and facing to be, and all other details right down to an estimate of the number of bricks.

With this in mind, find three good masons, those with reputations for building successful fireplaces right the first time, and ask each to bid on the job. Insist that they come to your home and see exactly where the fireplace will be installed. Show them your list of supplies and ask them to comment on it. Then ask them for a dollar estimate. You may be surprised at the range in their figures. A recent project we know of was estimated by three masons, and the highest bid was double that of the lowest.

This all-metal heat-circulating fireplace by Majestic is a metal form around which masonry is applied. Note intake and outtake grilles at left.

If you can, find out why there is great variation among the bids, for this may indicate certain areas where money may be saved. Perhaps one mason has to drive fifty miles each way while another lives around the corner. Perhaps one has another job close by and can order supplies for both fireplaces at once, saving on quantity. Perhaps one just charges more for working in the winter.

Be sure that your mason is willing to follow your specifications. Some masons think they know a lot more about fireplaces than Count Rumford did — at least until their fireplaces start to smoke. But few have had the experience Rumford had with fireplaces. So don't be talked out of your desire for Rumford proportions and principles.

Masons usually do not work alone; they hire helpers to work along with them to mix and bring mortar, to carry bricks, and to help in many other ways. Will your mason do the job for less if you help him? By doing so, you would also learn a great deal about putting up fireplaces.

Some masons make a profit on the supplies that are used as well as on the time spent in actual construction. But we know a mason who prefers not to purchase the supplies himself. He has the homeowner do that. He will, of course, indicate how much he needs of each item, but the homeowner pays the bill as the materials are delivered, so the mason is not short of cash.

If this arrangement is satisfactory with your mason, shop around on the market for the supplies you need and get the best at the best prices. Perhaps even trucking the supplies in yourself will be cheaper than having the supplier drop them off.

Sometimes the mason is the best person to ask for ideas on cost-saving. He may have ideas you might never think of, and no doubt he would be more current on best prices than most laymen since he is daily involved with masonry work. He should also be knowledgeable about the local building code. Ask him to name owners of other fireplaces he has built; then ask them what their cost experiences have been and how they would do it if they were starting all over again. This gives you another check on the ability and skills of your mason.

Of course if a fireplace can be anticipated when the plans for your home are being drawn up, the house framing plans can allow for the fireplace. New bracing, moving of conduits, new supports for load-bearing walls, and other time-consuming details can be eliminated or lessened if a fireplace is planned along with the house even though it is built some years later.

Don't forget to cost out alternatives. For instance, it might occur to you that fieldstone in your back yard would cost nothing and save on the cost of brick. Perhaps. But perhaps not. Building codes usually require that chimneys of stone be thicker than those of brick. This will require more mortar. And some of the stones will most certainly have to be dressed a bit. This will take time for which you will pay the mason. The foundation will have to be larger because the chimney will be larger; this will require more concrete. And just the matter of carrying the stones will require more time than carrying brick, and this will result in a longer time to build the fireplace. Since it takes longer to build with stone than with brick, be prepared for a larger labor bill. Perhaps it really is cheaper to use brick instead of fieldstone.

Massiveness of many stone fireplaces is lessened by light appearance of this stone, blending with walls of room. Portland Willamette Co. photo.

Just isolating the most costly element in constructing the fire-place and concentrating on ways to reduce that can turn up some surprising ways to save money — ways you might never have thought of otherwise. But there are a number of rather obvious ways cost-savings may be achieved.

Cement blocks, for instance, usually are less expensive than bricks. Where brick would be called for, but where brick would not be seen in your construction, why not use cement blocks? For instance, inside the outer brick wall of an exposed chimney, in the attic where the chimney passes to reach the roof (then continue with brick on the outside where the chimney is seen), and in back of the fire bricks in the fire chamber, and to support the back hearth? And, yes, even for some exposed walls such as the rear wall of the chimney in back of the fire chamber which often becomes the exposed wall of the adjoining room? Cement blocks are easily painted, and they don't really look bad at all as part of a wall in certain rooms such as dens and basements. Just be sure they have the proper strength and are suitable for this purpose. Your masonry supply house will be able to advise you.

Would you like some free bricks? Keep an eye open for brick buildings being torn down. You may be able to get bricks without cost, or for only a small charge. Good sound bricks can be used again. They have to be cleaned of the mortar that is stuck to them, and this is laborious and time-consuming. If you have the time and inclination, it is a good way to save money. Furthermore, there is nothing more delightful than a fireplace and chimney faced with used bricks. Good used bricks that have been cleaned ready for use are in demand and expensive. Get yours before they have been cleaned and save money.

Let's assume you have a raised hearth and the front hearth is supported by the foundation slab. Why make the raised front hearth a solid structure all the way through? Why not build it up with cement blocks and face it with bricks and let it be hollow inside? You will save quantities of brick. It is a simple procedure to lay the front hearth on top of this, and no one will know it isn't solid all the way through.

You may find that common bricks with one-inch holes in the center are less expensive than solid bricks. They are lighter to work with, and the holes make them very easy to set securely in mortar. Even if they cost only a couple of cents less than solid bricks, you may be able to save several dollars.

We strongly recommend building chimneys with flue liners, but we are realistic enough to know that some people build chimneys without them, and others will continue to do so.

"Choosing a kind of firewood to burn in your fireplace is much like selecting a favorite wine or cheese, since each wood species can offer something different in aroma or heat value. The fuelwood connoisseur will want to choose his wood carefully and weigh his needs and tastes before building his fire."

USDA Leaflet 559,
Firewood for Your Fireplace

55

Perhaps, depending on local conditions, you can save some money by eliminating flue liners; however, you will have to make the chimney walls thicker if you do, and this will require more masonry. Check it all out in detail first, for you may find that you actually save money in the long run by having them. Perhaps your insurance company will charge a higher premium if you do not have flue liners.

Using good-looking common brick for facing around the fireplace opening will probably save you a few dollars over using decorative facing. You can make your own rustic mantel from a tree you cut on your own land, or which you can get from the utility company when it prunes and before it carts the brush to the dump. This costs much less than buying one already seasoned and finished. Old barn beams are also very attractive as mantels.

And finally, most contractors have "off-season" periods when their rates are lower than when they are usually busier. Don't be afraid to ask masons if they have an off-season period and what their estimate would be if the fireplace were to be built then. You may have to wait a few weeks or a couple months, but the saving may be well worth it.

Homeowners often have "post mortems," to say how they would do something if they had it to do all over again, how they could have saved money if they had done such and such. Some post mortems are worthless; but homeowners, almost more than any other group, show a serious willingness to share their experiences with one another. So long as their post mortem advice does not encourage you to violate the basic principles of safe and sound fireplace building, and so long as it does not violate building codes, you may do well to consider some of the things they suggest. One important point, however: shortcuts do not always make permanent and safe savings, so be sure to consider all advice carefully and judge it against the safety of the long-term investment that a fireplace will add to the home.

"A house without woman and fire-light, is like a body without soul or sprite."

Benjamin Franklin,
from *Poor Richard's Almanac*

ADDING A CHIMNEY AND FIREPLACES

Second-floor bedroom fireplace.

A Practical Experience

By Marc Rogers

Peter and Elisabeth Holm have added fireplaces and a central chimney to an existing home. Ask them for advice on how to do it and Elisabeth will tell you, with a smile, "Find the best mason you can. Then move into the best motel you can find, and stay there until the work is done."

That's certainly not the way she and her radiologist-husband did it in their huge, rambling farmhouse in lovely Cornwall, Vermont.

They found the best mason around. But instead of living out, they lived in, with two sons, Anders, age 5, and Erik, age 2, assorted cats and dogs, and workmen, and neighbors dropping in to see what was going on. The Holms joined in the work, recognizing their lack of skills and choosing work of the strong back and stout heart variety.

They've liked the results, too. A huge Colonial fireplace in the kitchen, smaller, more formal fireplaces in the living room and dining room, and that special luxury, a fireplace in their second-floor bedroom, a huge room with arched ceiling. When, in the early 19th century, guests stepped from their stagecoaches into this inn, that room was the ballroom. All of these fireplaces look as if they belong right where they are, and had been there since the house was build in the 1790's by William Slade, father of a governor of Vermont.

The beginning of this fireplace story was in Charlotte, Vermont, where the Holms lived while Dr. Peter was completing his internship and residency at the Medical Center Hospital of Vermont in Burlington.

As the time came to move to the Middlebury area, where Peter would practice at the Porter Medical Center, the Holms made up their minds about their future home, deciding exactly what they wanted.

The house they found fitted the bill. It was old but still structurally sound. It was high on a hill, looking down over the Otter Creek valley. And it certainly hadn't been modernized. "It was really in pretty much of a shambles," recalls Elisabeth.

One curious change had been made in it. The house had been built with an immense central chimney from cellar through three floors to the roof, and with many a fireplace. A previous owner had torn out that big chimney and in its place had built a slim chimney for the coal furnace in the cellar. The roof had been built up to that chimney, but down below Elisabeth says, "there was a large hole from basement to attic."

Sensibly, there in the hot summer, they planned how they would renovate the house. They made a list of projects, and well down on that list was reconstruction of the chimney and the addition of fireplaces. That could wait.

Sensibly, again, in the cold winter, they changed those plans, as cold drafts raced from the basement to attic, and they found heating that gigantic cave was all but impossible. Reconstruction of the chimney was now at the top of the list. It couldn't wait.

Massive kitchen fireplace spreads its warmth and cheer.

During that chilly winter, as they tried to heat their new home with a coal furnace with three hot air vents, they did much of their preliminary planning.

Dr. Holm studied fireplace construction, particularly the work of Count Rumford, the American who redesigned the fireplace to win fame both in Europe and here.

They talked with William Ringey, a Cornwall man of many years and a photographic memory. Mr. Ringey had lived in the house as a boy, and remembered the fireplaces as they were before the chimney had been torn out. He could recall their sizes and their mantels.

They explored their own home, and the outbuildings, and the explorations were fruitful. Behind the hanging cupboards of their kitchen they found sections of the original pine paneling that had been above the fireplace. Some of it was broken, other sections had round holes, charred on the edges, where stovepipes had been run through into the chimney. But there was enough to salvage for use and to show the pattern that had been used.

The mantel for the dining room was out in the barn, in relatively good condition. And the antique crane for the kitchen fireplace was found there, too.

The big step was getting acquainted with Richard Bissonette of Vergennes, a mason with skill and experience, an interest in the project "and the patience of Job," says Mrs. Holm.

Bissonette and the Holms spent hours in planning, and those were hours well spent.

The Holms were going to replace most of the plumbing and wiring in the home, and found new pipes and wiring extending from one floor to the next could be incorporated into the chimney, and thus save cutting through the floors in other areas.

They made practical decisions during these hours. How many fireplaces? They decided to stick to the original house plan, as recalled by Mr. Ringey, and have three downstairs and one upstairs. But they did omit the one or two fireplaces that had been in the basement, and left out the dumb waiter that had run from the basement to the second-floor ballroom.

Should they install a Dutch oven? The original house had not had one, and they were constructing for maximum heat, not for beauty or display. The Dutch oven idea was scratched.

Should they use old bricks? It would be more expensive, and no more functional. They decided on old bricks only where they would show.

With all of those decisions made, with the shallow and slanted fireplaces of the Rumford design decided upon, Bissonette had blueprints made. They included five flues, four for the fireplaces and one for the new oil furnace-hot water system that was installed. And they planned another chimney, for a woodstove, in a section of the house not warmed by the radiation from any of the fireplaces.

Construction began in May, and Elisabeth's memory of the next six months is an album of sharp mental pictures.

The workmen poured a 14' × 18' concrete foundation, and Elisabeth remembers the river of concrete piped from the truck outside her back door, through her kitchen and down into the basement.

The walls of that foundation were built up of concrete block, and the resulting huge room was filled with rocks and rubble, all wheeled through the kitchen in wheelbarrows. She remembers the problems of finding enough rock and rubble, the never-ending trips of the wheelbarrows, the bone weariness that comes with moving some of those tons of rubble.

She watched with some doubt as this foundation was capped with concrete. It had to be

Dining by firelight possible in this dining room.

at just the right height or the brick hearths in the three downstairs rooms would not be level with the wide floorboards. (It came out exactly right.)

Thousands of old bricks were needed. But where to find them? Elisabeth remembers the mixed feelings she had when she learned an old home, a landmark in Middlebury, was being torn down; the sorrow because of the loss of the old building, the elation because of finding exactly the bricks needed, and in large numbers.

"And then, for months, we cleaned bricks. Muriatic acid and rubber gloves, day after day."

Then came another decision. Duplicate the paneling of old or use stock material? The Holms concluded that "this is no ego trip," so used stock, but had a Middlebury carver duplicate the missing pieces of the old dining room mantel.

Mrs. Holm thought, when the construction was planned, that she would stay well out of the way. But she didn't. "I couldn't just sit in a dirty kitchen and watch. I had never seen a chimney built and there was so much to learn. So I worked most of the time." And so did her husband, in his hours away from the hospital. They helped fill those empty spots with rubble, as the five flues were set with mortar, then rubble was placed between them and the outside bricks. They cleaned the old bricks and carried old bricks and new to where they were used, and some of those old bricks were used at the very top of the chimney, where it shows through about the roof.

Finally came that long-awaited day when the construction was completed. The last brick had been carried, the rubble was in place, and all of the dampers had been installed. The fireplaces were tried, and didn't smoke. It was a most satisfying day.

With the earlier sunsets, the frosts and soon the snow came a new period of learning — working with the fireplaces to get maximum heat.

60

"I had never had the comfort of fireplaces, so I was afraid at first," said Mrs. Holm. "Gradually I learned to control the dampers to get the most heat. And I saw how the big chimney would store heat during the day and release it gradually during the night."

Very soon a fire in the kitchen fireplace became a daily event, burning from before breakfast until bedtime. Mrs. Holm learned to let the fire burn down to a bed of coals in the evening, then place a black aluminum "snuffer" over that bed. In that way the damper of the fireplace can be closed, halting the flow of hot air up and out of the chimney during the night. The kitchen is roomy and comfortable, a natural gathering place. The fire in the fireplace added to its lure.

On the efficiency of fireplaces, Mrs. Holm says stoutly, "They're very much maligned. They are, of course, not as efficient as stoves but they can add a lot of heat to a home. And the comfort of them. You can walk up to a fireplace, sit by it and get warm, and have its light."

The Holms have thought about what they learned from building this chimney, and one of the lessons Elisabeth learned is:

"We would never try to build one ourselves. I tried laying a few bricks, with a mason watching and helping me, and it's not easy to get them straight. I have all the respect in the world for artisans and the work they do."

They strongly urge others to find a mason, a good mason whose work can be seen and judged, then trust him on many of the decisions. The Holms recall how they wanted a slate hearth build a certain way. Richard Bissonette was most pleasant about it, but simply refused to build it, telling them they would be disappointed because it would crack. They are glad now they went along with his decision.

Arched fireplace adds beauty to living room.

Would they take on such a construction job again?

They hesitate in answering that question. Elisabeth thinks of the many days when her kitchen was a highway for a line of wheelbarrows, when home life was disrupted by rubble to move and bricks to clean, and she suggests the advantages of motel life to get away from construction.

But then she sits by that big, comfortable table in front of the kitchen fireplace, and its flames cast changing lights on her face.

She thinks of the work she did, glancing over the familiar old bricks she cleaned and carried, the crane she found, the firewood she piled in the kitchen, and then answers, "I guess I like it, having had a part in building it, and now having an old house that we have contributed to."

Kitchen fireplace is most used of all.

"There are enough fagots and waste wood of all kinds in the forests of most of our towns to support many fires, but which at present warm none, and, some think, hinder the growth of the young wood."

Henry D. Thoreau,
Walden

6 Getting More Heat From the Fireplace

While it is recognized that a fireplace is not the most efficient heater for the home (approximately 90 percent of the heat goes up the chimney), attempts have been made and are still being made to capture the lost heat and use it to lower the heating bill.

"... Having, in 1742, invented an open stove for the better warming of rooms, and at the same time saving fuel, as the fresh air was warmed in entering, I made a present of the model to Mr. Robert Grace, one of my early friends, who having an iron furnace found the casting of the plates for these stoves a profitable thing, as they were growing in demand. To promote that demand I wrote and published a pamphlet entitled 'An Account of the new-invented Pennsylvanian Fire-places, wherein their Construction and Manner of Operation are particularly explained, their advantages above every other Method of Warming Rooms demonstrated, and all Objections that have been raised against the Use of them answered and obviated,' etc. This pamphlet had a good effect. Governor Thomas was so pleased with the construction of this stove, as described in it, that he offered to give me a patent for the sole vending of them for a term of years, but I declined it from a principle which has ever weighed with me on such occasions, viz., that as we enjoy great advantages from the inventions of others, we should be glad of an opportunity to serve others by any invention of ours, and this we should do freely and generously."

Benjamin Franklin,
Autobiography

Count Rumford, realizing that the heat coming from a fireplace into a room is radiant heat, sloped the fireback and angled the covings to throw the maximum amount of radiant heat out from the fireplace.

Benjamin Franklin was concerned about the problem even before Count Rumford, and he attempted to do something about it when he developed the Pennsylvanian fireplace. This was probably the first successful heat-circulating fireplace even though it was not widely used. He described it in a pamphlet published in 1744, "An Account of the New-Invented Pennsylvanian Fire-places."

Franklin's Pennsylvanian fireplace was made of six cast-iron plates, fastened together with rods. It could be opened at the front, like a conventional fireplace, and had a short hood-like front plate across the top of this front. A quick glance would lead the viewer to conclude this was only a cast iron fireplace, or open stove.

There were two major differences. One was that Franklin installed in the stove a narrow baffle box that spanned the width of the stove. This was completely enclosed from the air circulating in the fire. Air came into this box from the outside through a hole in the bottom, and the heated air passed out through holes in the upper sides of the stove.

The second fundamental difference was that the air entered the stove from the bottom, was heated in the flames, then, with the smoke, had to pass up, over and down the rear of the baffle box, heating it and the air in it, then pass out the bottom of the stove.

All air for Pennsylvanian fireplace came from outside source (lower left). Air feeding flames passed up and over baffle box, then smoke and air went under brick wall and into chimney. Air going into baffle box was heated, then passed out into the room through holes in the upper parts of the sides of the fireplace.

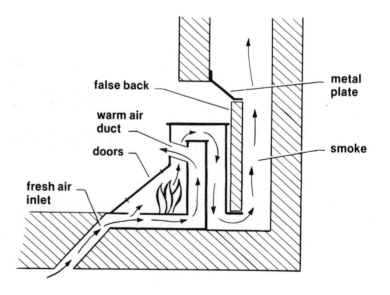

And how did the air and smoke get out? The installation of the stove, a complicated job, provided for it. The stove was built to be installed in a conventional fireplace. But the home-owner had to build another brick wall, behind the stove location and completely blocking off all entrance to the chimney. Behind this wall was an air space leading up into the chimney.

Next he had to dig several holes. One led from a source of fresh air, such as outdoors or the cellar, into the baffle box. And the second one led from the bottom of the stove under the new wall and into the air space leading to the chimney — the route for the smoke to travel.

While the principle of the baffle box is much the same as is used in today's heat-circulating fireplaces, there are reasons for believing that Franklin's stove or fireplace was not a heated success. History indicates that many of them were modified by removing the baffle box, and others were changed so that the smoke could rise through a hole in the rear top of the stove.

This unit was invented many years before Franklin designed the Franklin stove, which was a stove designed to burn pitcoal.

In recent years there have been a number of attempts to capture more heat from the fireplace. They vary from prefabricated metal forms for the fire chamber unit with vents to circulate the warm air, to fire grates or log irons for circulating heat. These attempts to get more heat from the fireplace have nearly all been concerned with getting this heat through convection — either through natural convection by heated air rising or through mechanical assistance, such as the use of fans to move the air through heated chambers or against heated surfaces and then circulating it throughout the room.

Let us look at some of these.

"If you have a fireplace, the best attitude in the long run may be to sublimate thoughts about its inefficiency and enjoy this luxury for what it does offer."

Larry Gay,
The Complete Book of Heating with Wood

By "modified fireplaces" we usually mean those that have a large prefabricated metal unit around which bricks are laid to give the appearance of a conventional fireplace. The prefabricated unit is one that contains the fire chamber, the damper, the throat, the smoke shelf, and a large smoke chamber. Various parts, such as the sides and back of the fire chamber, are of double-wall construction to provide warming ovens for cool air. Baffles are frequently built into the unit to prolong the exposure of cool air to heat. Manufacturers claim that its proportions are correct, and that a smokeless fireplace is virtually assured. Warm air is expelled from the top of the unit

MODIFIED FIREPLACES

Such units as this are free-standing or fit in a fireplace. Cool air is drawn into the bottom of the unit, expelled through vents in the top.

through registers to heat the room; or it may be channeled to vents in adjacent rooms or even to rooms upstairs.

One must provide the same type of foundation for a modified fireplace as for a conventional one. And furthermore, the chimney and its flue require the same construction as would be required for a conventional fireplace.

Modified fireplaces radiate heat, and since they are designed especially to circulate heat, they are more efficient than a conventional fireplace in this respect.

But there are other things you should consider.

The cost of a fireplace may or may not be greater if you use a prefabricated metal unit. If you are not doing the work yourself and have to pay for labor, the prefabricated unit may represent a saving. Costing this out before construction starts will indicate whether there are savings to be achieved.

Some masons refuse to work on these fireplaces. They believe it is possible with masonry alone to provide for similar or just as efficient heat-circulation ducts as one gets with a prefabricated unit (but likely not so quickly since it takes longer to heat masonry than it does to heat metal).

They may also have doubts about the durability of the metal unit. Check out how resistant the metal unit is to corrosion caused by smoke and gases from the fire. Does the manufacturer guarantee that corrosion will not occur? And for how long?

Check with your mason on his experiences. Check with several persons who have installed such fireplaces. The manufacturer should be able to supply names; so should your mason.

There are several makes of modified fireplace units on the market. Look into them thoroughly before you buy.

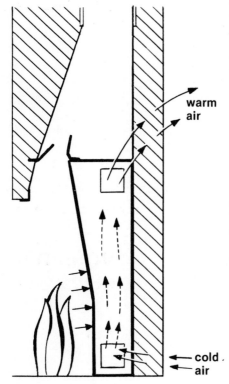

Common heating system draws cool air in at bottom, warms it in enclosed area behind flames, expels it at top.

warm air

cold air

Some of these fireplaces have electric fans installed within the air ducts to increase the flow of air through the unit and to circulate it faster into the room.

Discuss with your supplier the proper size of the prefabricated fireplace you will need. He will take into account the amount of space you wish to heat. Plan well ahead so the air ducts from the fireplace to the rooms you wish to heat will vent where you want them to.

These modified fireplaces can be made to look just as attractive as conventional ones. Except for the air vents, one might not suspect at all that they are modified fireplaces.

An additional touch might be to install a large metal hood from the top of the fireplace opening to perhaps the ceiling. This could conceal the warm-air outlets above the fireplace opening, and warm air could then circulate up under the hood and out through its sides or top.

Heating Water to Circulate Air

Attempts have been made to circulate water through copper piping that is heated in the rear of the fire chamber or in the flue itself. The hot water is then conducted to a radiator which warms the air similar to normal water-heating systems. Grates have also been made of tubular metal through which the water flows as it is heated. Several of these experiments have been fairly successful, and we may expect to see other inventions on the market from time to time that heat water which warms air for circulation.

Additional Heat from Fireplace Grates

Considerable experimentation has been given to grates that would increase heat from the fireplace.

One such development has been a grate raised and tilted so the fire and coals are better exposed to radiate heat.

Yet another development has been a grate made of tubular metal. Several lengths shaped like bows are fastened vertically to a base. Logs are laid on the bottom curve of these bows, heating air within them. An electric blower is sometimes added to force air into the lower ends of the bows and on out the open tops after it is heated. Simple and quite efficient, this development of the grate may be used also with Franklin stoves to increase heating efficiency.

A recent invention to get more heat from the fireplace also involves a grate that is similar to andirons. A large log is placed toward the back with several smaller ones toward the front.

67

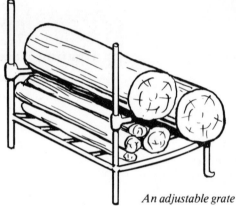

An adjustable grate

An adjustable arm slides down vertical extensions at the front of each end of the grate until it touches the large log. Then a log somewhat smaller in thickness than the large one is placed on these arms to locate it right over the two smaller logs that are on the bottom of the grate. This makes a definite space between the top log and the two smaller ones beneath. As a consequence this space becomes a sort of furnace, storing heat and sending it forth into the room. It is reported that about 30 percent of the heat from this cavity is radiated into the room (a good increase over the normal amount). Furthermore, this cavity or slot greatly increases the ease of kindling the fire. This invention is called the "Texas Fireframe," since it was invented by a physicist from Texas.

The Finns are well known for the massive masonry structures they build within their homes — structures which may incorporate several fireplaces as well as ovens, seats, and sleeping platforms. Such a structure enables them to use the maximum amount of heat they can capture from a fire. Not only does the fireplace give off radiant heat, but the heat is conducted by the masonry throughout the structure (which makes it warm to sleep on) and air coming in contact with the heated masonry circulates convected heat. Of course the great weight of these structures requires an enormous footing to support it. But since the climate of Finland requires that fires burn constantly throughout the long and bitter winters, these large structures which hold the heat and release it gradually make a lot of sense.

With the great concern today for conserving energy and reducing the cost of heating, we may expect to see many new ideas forthcoming for capturing and utilizing the enormous amount of heat that is wasted when we build a fire.

It is interesting to speculate on what could be done to increase the heating efficiency of the fireplace. The following sketch* gives an idea of some possibilities.

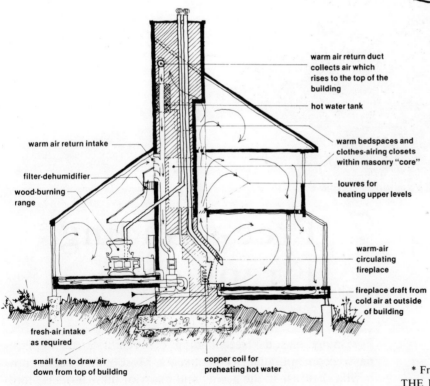

warm air return duct collects air which rises to the top of the building

hot water tank

warm air return intake

warm bedspaces and clothes-airing closets within masonry "core"

filter-dehumidifier

louvres for heating upper levels

wood-burning range

warm-air circulating fireplace

fireplace draft from cold air at outside of building

fresh-air intake as required

small fan to draw air down from top of building

copper coil for preheating hot water

* From Peter Clegg: ENERGY FOR THE HOME, *page 217,* published 1975 by Garden Way Publishing Company, Charlotte, Vermont 05445

69

7 Free-standing Fireplaces

For many reasons free-standing or prefabricated fireplaces have become popular in recent years. Most building codes now permit their use in the home, and many of these models, complete with their chimney units, have been approved by Underwriters Laboratories.

Their popularity has many explanations. Each is usually a complete self-contained unit with everything that is needed for installation, except perhaps the hearth. But even the flue, the housing, and whatever is required for the chimney are in the kit.

These assemblies are light in weight and require no heavy foundation in most instances, certainly never one that would come anywhere near the weight or the cost of that required for a masonry fireplace.

Usually of ceramic or metal construction, they come in so many styles and colors that they are limited only by the manufacturer's imagination. Do you want the opening on the right side or on the left? Or perhaps on the front? Would you prefer one that swivels? And would you like to use electricity instead of wood for the "fire"? Or perhaps LP or natural gas? You have your choice.

The skill required for installation is minimal, and many can be installed in a single day, the most difficult part of the job being cutting through the roof for the chimney.

An ordinary (or uninsulated) stove pipe may be used to vent the smoke into an existing chimney. Or you may use the prefabricated chimney that comes with most of the fireplaces and which can easily be angled around an obstruction. They are light in weight, being usually double steel chimneys separated by insulation, or else an outer chimney of some type of incombustible metal with a terra-cotta liner for the flue. The latter are frequently referred to as "patent" chimneys. While it is sometimes a little more convenient to use a conventional flue, it is best to use the flue that comes with the prefabricated fireplace to be sure that conditions of the manufacturer's warranty will not be violated. Read the warranty well.

These fireplaces may be located almost everywhere in the house, free-standing or even hung from the wall or ceiling or set on a raised hearth. Those who remember the long stove pipes in the old country stores will find a similarity here, for the chimneys may be exposed for long stretches to give off more heat. Some, such as the Franklin stove, may be placed within the fire chamber of a conventional fireplace.

In terms of cost, the free-standing fireplace represents a big savings over masonry fireplaces, perhaps as much as two-thirds or more.

In general they give off more heat than the conventional fireplace. This is especially true of those models with metal hoods which radiate heat. Others act similarly to the modified fireplaces we discussed in Chapter 6, for they have been de-

"Some brittle sticks of thorn or briar
Make me a fire,
Close by whose living coal I sit,
And glow like it."

Robert Herrick,
A Thanksgiving to God for His House

71

signed to circulate heat by the use of baffles and metal air-warming chambers.

Why, then, would anyone prefer a traditional masonry fireplace to a free-standing prefabricated one? There are several reasons.

Perhaps it is psychological, but if one has been brought up in a home with a conventional fireplace, or if one has experienced its warmth and charm anywhere, there is something about the masonry fireplace that is soul-satisfying and complete, something that cannot be shared with anything except a masonry fireplace. It represents something permanent and sound; it is not ersatz in any way. It is a substitute for nothing; it is IT, the real thing!

Furthermore, it adds much more to the value of a home than does the prefabricated fireplace. It is a permanent fixture whereas the prefabricated one is movable and is thought of as being more of a temporary fireplace.

The conventional fireplace is far less apt to smoke from sudden drafts or from people passing by than is the free-standing type. A good draft is mandatory with free-standing models, especially the type that is open all the way around. An air conduit from the outside to the firebox may be necessary for an adequate draft, possibly even augmented by a fan.

A plain corner is turned into a cheerful center of attraction by this fireplace.

Many free-standing fireplaces are fabricated with multiple walls, between which air circulates to keep the outer wall cool. Others have insulation between the walls for the same purpose. As a result, it is not always necessary to provide a great amount of clearance when locating the fireplace. But from the point of view of draft it is best to place it several feet from doors, windows, and walls. You should follow the instructions of the manufacturer precisely as to clearance and other details when assembling the unit. If you don't, you may find that the warranty will not be honored if something goes wrong. For this reason, it is best to purchase the entire assembly from the same source and not make do with home-made substitutes for any integral part of it. The local building code, too, should be followed. In the event the code does not allow the manufacturer's instructions to be followed, try to get a variance or else determine from the manufacturer whether he will honor the warranty if the local building code is followed instead. Before purchasing the unit, ask the manufacturer or supplier for a copy of the instructions for assembling it. This will give you more time to plan and study the instructions.

Regardless of where the fireplace is located, it will be necessary to have some kind of hearth. This is simple to prepare, for the hearth can be built directly over the subfloor. Such non-combustible materials as brick, terra cotta, slate, ceramic tile and perhaps several inches of small pebbles inside a brick framework will be all the instructions call for. The fireplace unit will then sit on or be hung over this hearth. The hearth should extend about twenty inches in front of the fireplace and at least ten inches on all sides.

If your free-standing fireplace has a mantel or frame, the mantel should, as on a conventional fireplace, be a foot above the opening if it extends outward 1½ inches, and care should be taken to assure that any combustible material not be closer than 3½ inches from the opening if the fireplace has a frame or combination frame and mantel.

While the fireplace kit usually will contain the required assembly parts, you may have to purchase some materials for the chimney separately since not all chimneys will be the same length, and manufacturers usually supply only an average amount in a standard kit. But for reasons mentioned earlier, it is best to buy additional materials from the same source.

Since one of the main problems faced with free-standing fireplaces is smoking, there must be plenty of draft. And down-draft must be prevented. The instructions may suggest a chimney cap to prevent down-drafts, and possibly an air intake near

LOCATING AND INSTALLING

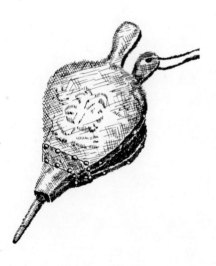

"The next winter I used a small cooking-stove for economy, since I did not own the forest; but it did not keep fire so well as the open fireplace. Cooking was then, for the most part, no longer a poetic, but merely a chemic process. It will soon be forgotten, in these days of stoves, that we used to roast potatoes in the ashes, after the Indian fashion. The stove not only took up room and scented the house, but it concealed the fire, and I felt as if I had lost a companion. You can always see a face in the fire. The laborer, looking into it at evening, purifies his thoughts of the dross and earthiness which they have accumulated during the day."

Henry D. Thoreau,
Walden

the base of the fire chamber for adequate air to feed the fire. Of course the taller the flue, the smaller are the chances for a smoke problem.

The diameter of the flue is important, too. Follow the recommendation of the manufacturer unless local building codes mandate otherwise. In the event neither suggests the size of the flue to use (very unlikely), check the Universal Building Code for directions. This should be available in your local library.

For fireplaces having a separate hood raised above the open fire chamber, it is especially important that the flue area be large enough. A good rule-of-thumb is to measure the distance from the hood to the rim of the fire chamber, then multiply this by the circumference of the hood and take 1/8th of this number. This is the minimum area of a cross-section of the flue liner.

The manufacturer's instructions and the local building code should specify the size of the enclosure that must be built around the chimney. This enclosure must prevent the chimney itself from coming in contact with any combustible material throughout its entire length. It must also provide for support of the chimney. Sections of chimney, usually supplied with a liner built within and insulated from the outer shell of the chimney, will fit securely together and lock with a twist. If obstructions are encountered while locating the chimney, it is a simple thing to use joint sections to circumvent the obstructions and continue on up to and through the roof.

The matter of cutting through the roof is similar to what was described in Chapter 4 when we were concerned with conventional fireplaces. Instructions with the assembly will specify what bracing and what clearances are necessary for the chimney as it goes through and on up above the roof.

The section above the roof may be left exposed or it may be enclosed in a fake outer chimney — really a wooden frame that is enclosed to look like a normal fireplace chimney, even painted to represent red bricks. Such fake chimneys sometimes extend all the way up the side of the house if they are designed to represent the outside chimney of a conventional fireplace that is set into the lower wall of the house. Have your fire department and insurance company approve this type of chimney before you install it.

The cast iron Franklin stove may be thought of as a prefabricated metal fireplace. This, too, requires no heavy foundation but rather a fire-proof hearth with insulation properties such as we have mentioned above for prefabricated fireplaces. They may be vented directly into existing unused flues or they may have prefabricated or patent chimneys installed.

Logs burn well in these fireplaces, and the metal gives off an abundance of radiant heat. The different models of the Franklin stove are legion, some provided with all the appurtenances to fit into any desired style or decoration. Optional parts and adornments are frequently for sale as add-ons; however, it is best to purchase additional parts from the same manufacturer who made the stove, for there are many different manufacturers, and all parts are not interchangeable with the stoves of other manufacturers.

We think of the Franklin stove as a substitute for a fireplace, yet the models that have doors are actually closed stoves when the doors are swung shut.

The Pennsylvanian fireplace was a forerunner of today's units to fit into fireplaces.

The Atlanta Stove Works Franklin stove has doors that can be closed, for safety or to provide more heat.

Another type of metal stove that has fireplace properties is represented by the famous Norwegian Jøtul stove. As a stove, it is one of the greatest heaters on the market. The interior baffles that circulate the smoke and gases for additional heat also contribute to the efficient slow-burning of the logs. And circulating air is warmed on the outside and spread throughout the rooms.

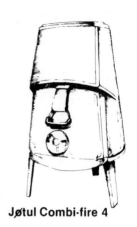

Jøtul Combi-fire 4

When the front door is closed, the Jøtul performs as a stove. But the front door is on tracks which allow it to be swung open and stored under the fire chamber, thus opening the front to expose the fire and become, in effect, a fireplace. Both radiant heat and circulating heat pour forth from the stove at the same time. Smoke and gases can be vented through an ordinary flue, or the opening of a regular fireplace can be closed with sheet metal during the winter, and a flue from the stove through an opening in the sheet metal can direct the smoke and gases into the fireplace chamber. From there the fireplace flue vents the smoke and gases to the outside of the house.

Warning

In spite of what we have said above about foundations for free-standing fireplaces, we are still greatly concerned about the potential fire danger of an insufficiently designed foundation, especially if the fireplace is likely to be used over sustained periods of time. As we remarked earlier, the sustained use of a fireplace can ignite floors and floor joists that a short, hotter fire would never set. With all due respect to manufacturer's instructions and building codes, we would feel much safer if everyone installing a free-standing fireplace would consult with his local fire chief first for advice on the type and thickness of the foundation. He certainly will suggest nothing less than the manufacturer or the building code. If he recommends more, follow his instructions. His experience investigating fires should initiate some good counsel that will prevent other fires.

"Fire and people do in this agree,
They both good servants,
    both ill masters be."

Fulke Greville, First Baron Brooke,
Inquisition upon Fame

76

8 Styles and Designs

We have already explained the importance of building the fireplace and chimney with proportions and dimensions that will insure a warm, smokeless fire. However, once these specifications have become part of your plan, there is almost no limit to the materials which may be used; the size, shape, and ornamentations of the fireplace, and even its location, are up to you.

Before deciding on the style of your fireplace, ask yourself what you want from a fireplace and how you will be using it. Is your life style formal or informal? Do you entertain crowds of people, or small intimate groups? Is the fireplace to be the main source of heat, or is it mainly for the enjoyment of the cheerful flames?

The architectural style of your home and your type of furniture could influence the style you choose for the fireplace. A log cabin furnished with early American or colonial furniture would beckon for a colonial type fireplace, whereas a very modern home would need a modern style to match. A ski lodge or beach house might call for a different style from a year-round home in the suburbs or city.

And finally, you must decide whether the fireplace is to be the dominant feature, or whether it should blend in with the rest of the room.

There are many possible types of fireplaces. They may be of masonry, built into the house to your specifications, or they may be prebuilt, requiring only installation.

As to its size, that depends on its location in the room, the size of the room, and whether it is to be your principal source of heat.

LOCATION

Few objects have the versatility for location as does the fireplace. It can be built against an outside wall of the house with the chimney outside, or it can be built into an inside wall with an interior chimney. It can be in a corner, in a window wall, or in almost any room of the house. It is also possible to have two or three fireplaces sharing the same chimney (each with its own flue) either on different floors or opening on different sides of the same walls.

Whether flush with the wall or projecting into the room, the fireplace's front hearth will always jut into the room. The fireplace itself can sometimes take up a considerable amount of space in the room. When built on an outside wall, much of it can be planned to protrude outside the house, whereas when built on an inside wall, it has to take up space somewhere — either in the main room or in an adjacent room that it can be "backed" into. In this latter case, the size of the two rooms and their use would influence the location.

When a fireplace protrudes into a room, it is sometimes possible to build storage cabinets or shelves along each side, or to make it part of a long storage wall.

Of course if heating vents are being used, you will need to plan for their location.

With fireplaces built along an exterior wall, the chimney will determine whether the fireplace will be flush or projecting inside.

Never locate a fireplace in the line of traffic if it can be avoided. There should be space in front of the fire for chairs so people can sit, relax and watch the fire. And care should be taken to locate it where it will not be subject to drafts from windows and doors, as drafts will affect the performance of the fire.

Perhaps you plan to have some large pieces of furniture in the same room, such as a grand piano. Consider what problems, if any, this will cause. Do you wish to have two focal points in the same room, or do you want the room arranged so the large objects may blend together to form a single unit?

Are you torn between the desire to look at the view from your window and the desire to watch the flames flickering above the hearth? It is possible to do both. Simply locate the fireplace in the middle of the window wall, or else flank it with windows. Then when you don't want the view, draperies pulled over the windows can blot it out in an instant. Locating the fireplace in this manner means that you can have one furniture grouping for both the view and the fireplace instead of two different arrangements. Or a fireplace in the corner of two window walls will allow for a panoramic view with the fire in the center. Another possibility is to install windows over the fireplace. In that case you would see its outside chimney through the window, or, in the event of free-standing fireplaces, the prefabricated or patent chimney could by-pass the windows.

Sometimes a corner location appears to be a natural spot for a fireplace. There are no blind spots, and benches and sofas

along the walls are close enough to receive light and heat from the fire.

Occasionally people wish to have two or more fireplaces. If a common chimney can be used, there is of course some cost saving; otherwise separate chimneys would be required. It is possible to angle two fireplaces into a corner back to back, or they could be side by side with openings on different sides of the wall. It is even possible to have the same fireplace open on two sides into different rooms for a "see through" effect. This may pose problems with drafts, and a glass screen to shut off one fireplace while the other is being used is a good investment. Of course, the easiest way for two fireplaces to share the same chimney is to have one above the other on different floors, in which case the upstairs fireplace should be smaller than the lower one because its flue would be shorter.

Another possible consideration is a double fireplace opening into the living room or kitchen on one side and onto a patio or porch on the other. A back-to-back arrangement for this would be more efficient than a "see through" effect.

In general masonry fireplaces that are built to be open on two, yes, even on three, sides, while they have the advantage of being viewed from many angles, have less protection from cross drafts, and they frequently require special flues and dampers. In calculating the flue size, the total area of all the open faces must be considered and the damper must be especially designed for this type of fireplace. Again, we advocate glass screens on all but one side to allow it to perform like a conventional fireplace if there are smoke problems.

A free-standing fireplace is one of the most dramatic types available and is especially suited for ski lodges and beach houses. It, too, can be located almost anywhere, but it is not without a problem: the problem being to supply the fire with enough air and yet prevent air currents from deflecting smoke into the room. Some experts recommend an air duct from outside to supply adequate oxygen. Fans in the flue are sometimes able to control the smoke.

A masonry hood over a free-standing fireplace will require corner supports, but most free-standing fireplaces have metal hoods that can be hung from the wall or ceiling. The rims of these hoods should extend beyond the circumference of the firepit somewhat; and they should have a slope of at least 45 degrees. The hearth should also extend beyond the circumference of the firepit. These two points must be considered when locating a fireplace and planning for furniture arrangements.

"Keep the home fires burning,
   while your hearts are yearning,
Though your lads are far away
   they dream of home."

Lena Guilbert Ford,
Keep the Home Fires Burning

The materials used inside the fire chamber are pretty much limited to firebrick, steel, and soapstone.

However the materials used on the front of the fireplace — the facing — can vary greatly and can be handled in many different ways. Your choice is limited only by personal preference, overall architecture considerations, textures, colors, and the material available in your community.

Take concrete, for example. It may be used by itself or with adobe, exposed aggregate, quartz chips or terrazzo. And when it is applied, it may be troweled, floated, brushed, fluted, precast, hammered, ground, or polished.

Or you could use stone: marble, granite, limestone, slate, soapstone, or fieldstone, all of which may be split face, ground face, polished, carved, carved and polished, or glazed. This in turn may be laid in different patterns with a variety of bonds, joints and mortars.

Or the fireplace may be finished in metal such as iron, steel, stainless steel, aluminum, copper, brass or bronze; and these metals could be hammered, polished, embossed, cast, brushed, anodized, or figured.

Another possibility would be the use of ceramics such as quarry tile, terra cotta, glazed tile, mosaic tile, or glass. And they all can be decorated in different colors, shapes, sizes, textures, and patterns.

Brick probably is the most versatile material for facing since it comes in many colors and there are different ways of laying it, which makes it formal or informal. Just plain common brick, which is rough and porous, is sometimes used as facing when an informal or rustic effect is desired, or when the fireplace is to be painted.

Then there is face brick, brick with a hard surface and made especially for facing and exteriors. If an informal or an early American interior is to be matched with brick, very often used brick, with bits of old mortar still adhering to it, is most appropriate. Roman brick, which is often used in modern interiors, has a long narrow shape which makes for strong horizontal lines.

Brick does not have to be laid in monotonous courses. In order to make brickwork more interesting, it can be laid vertically or in such patterns as herringbone, criss cross, or basket weave. There are other styles and patterns as well.

It is possible to use stone picked up around your own property if you live in a rocky area. However, it is difficult to dress such stones and to fit them together properly, and some masons refuse to work with them.

"I lament the loss your town has suffered this year by fire. I sometimes think men do not act like reasonable creatures, when they build for themselves combustible dwellings, in which they are every day obliged to use fire. In my new buildings, I have taken a few precautions, not generally used; to wit, none of the wooden work of one room communicates with the wooden work of any other room; and all the floors, and even the steps of the stairs, are plastered close to the boards, besides the plastering on the laths under the joists. There are also trap-doors to go out upon the roofs, that one may go out and wet the shingles in case of a neighbouring fire."

Benjamin Franklin,
letter to Mrs. Jane Mecom in Philadelphia

Adobe lends a western touch to a fireplace. Frequently the fireplace is located in an adobe wall, in which case it is plastered and painted although it can be left natural. Or the fireplace can be faced with adobe and set in a wall of rustic paneling.

Wood panel facing is very popular, and it adds a warmth and textured interest. Depending on the style of the house, there is a wide choice of carved colonial panels, rough barn siding, knotty pine and redwood, to give just a few examples. When a combustible material such as wood is used for facing, it should not come within six inches of the opening of the fireplace.

HEARTH

The front hearth of the fireplace, especially of the masonry fireplace, offers many possibilities for the interior decorator. The hearth extends at least twenty inches from the fireplace opening and at least six inches from the sides of the opening, so its design becomes a very important consideration when planning the room. Brick, stone, terra cotta, slate, concrete, marble, and other fireproof materials are used to form the basis for many designs and finishes that tie the front hearth into the decorating scheme of the room.

The hearth can be made to cover even more area than is really necessary, almost forming a room within a room. Or it can be extended along the wall to form a band which ties the masonry into the room.

Raised hearths often make the fire more intimate as well as easier to see, especially in a dining or game room. Built to look solid, or cantilevered from the fire chamber, the raised hearth offers many possibilities. When it is not built solid or is cantilevered, it offers a convenient place to store firewood and kindling. And when built of material that contrasts with the facing, it gives a dramatic effect to the room.

Occasionally the back and front hearths will be built lower than the floor of the room. Such sunken hearths permit seating or conversation centers around them. But since the sunken hearth can be a hazard, it is well to consider a guard rail or a divider element to lessen the risk of people falling on it.

MANTELS

The mantel historically was the shelf over the fireplace. However, today it has taken on a fuller meaning to include sometimes the frame that often borders the facing of the fireplace. In the early days when the fireplace was used for cooking, the mantel was a necessary fixture as it could be used for keeping food warm and for storing pots and seasonings. When stoves replaced fireplaces for cooking, mantels became useful for decoration or as a place to keep a clock. Now they are often omitted, especially in houses of modern design.

The design of the mantel should harmonize with the style of the room. Its material and shape can tie the fireplace and the wall together. Sometimes a change in the mantel can change the whole appearance of a room, even the style. Just think about the possibilities that exist between a rough beam and a slab of marble or granite. And they may be fashioned into different shapes and with carvings or ornamentation. They may be purchased ready-made or custom-made, and the possibilities for their use are limitless. Some are so valuable that they have been used as special gifts and have become the prized possessions of the recipient, such as a mantel in the White House which was presented by the Queen of England.

The period styles are legion: French, Victorian, Regency, English Georgian, Spanish, Italian, and American Colonial, to name but a few. Adam mantels, designed by the Adam brothers of England in the eighteenth century, are highly decorated with scrolls, frets, carved ribbons, bows, and swags, and are greatly prized.

HOODS

A hood over the opening of the masonry fireplaces has become a sort of substitute for the mantel, and of course it is very common over the firepit of the free-standing models. Whether it projects from the wall or is suspended from the ceiling, whether traditional or freely designed, the hood, with its shape and texture, adds warmth and interest to the room.

Its presence also contributes to the heating efficiency of the fireplace since it radiates heat that is finding its way up the chimney, and the heat of the hood encourages greater air circulation up the flue.

Copper, stainless steel, and aluminum are common metals used for hoods. The natural finish of copper is greatly desired, for it can be oxidized to a greenish hue or polished. Other metals can be painted bright or given an antique finish. Texturing by hammering, sandblasting, etching, polishing, or tooling expands the adaptability of these metals for decorating plans.

WALLS

We have already discussed the possibility of putting a fireplace in a window wall. It is equally attractive against a blank wall. Then the mantel and hearth line can be continued around the wall to become the tops of built-in bookcases and storage shelves. Books and fire seem to go together, and the pattern of books on the shelves flanking the fireplace seems to repeat the pattern of the brick work and makes a pleasing effect. However, if the fireplace is used a great deal and the chimney stays warm near the books, they will tend to dry out unless rotated.

When a fireplace is used as a partition between two rooms, the masonry around it can be built to become a wall, which need not be of ceiling height, or another fireplace can be built opening into the other room. The wall on either side of the fireplace can also be designed for storage.

Entire wall of masonry can give pleasing effect (Portland Willamette Co. photo).

Since extensive solid masonry walls tend to become deadening, it is wise to have variations in patterns especially if an entire wall is an extension of the fireplace masonry. Paneling can also be used to relieve any sameness in masonry. Bricks laid in basket weave, mortared with wide joints, or stacked, can produce interesting effects as can variations in color. Sometimes stone, instead of brick, brings a welcome relief.

ORNAMENTATION

Mantels, hoods, and fireplace accessories can provide ornamentation for the fireplace. However, even a plain mantel can be made ornamental by the objects put on it or over it. We usually think of a clock or candlesticks on the mantel and a landscape or portrait over it; but there is no limit to the interesting and beautiful objects which one may display. Sculptures, mirrors, collages, rugs, tapestries, collections of various sorts are all possibilities — whatever you enjoy displaying and looking at.

FURNITURE

Furniture should be arranged so that people can relax around the fire without having traffic come between it and them. However, be sure to leave enough room so the fire-tender can get in and out without trampling on people. Simple arrangements of furniture are squares, rectangles, half circles, full circles, and L-shapes.

SAFETY

First and last with fireplaces we have to think of safety. But because they are so versatile and present so many possibilities for the home decorator, there is no reason to tempt fate by violating any of the common rules and guidelines of safety first. There will still be alternatives and other options to provide satisfaction for even the most discriminating.

9 How to Stop a Fireplace from Smoking

When a fire is first lighted in the fireplace, a bit of smoke may escape into the room, especially if the chimney is cold. Outside chimneys are more apt to be cold than those built entirely within the house. So first hold a lighted newspaper up inside the fire chamber near the open damper; its quick flame will turn around almost any down-draft, and as the fire burns below, the up-draft should improve as the chimney heats up.

Even so, there can be no guarantee that a fireplace will not smoke even though it has been built with the utmost care. But if it has been built properly and with the Rumford principles observed, the chances that it will smoke have been reduced to a minimum; and the causes of its smoking should not be found within the structure of the fireplace and chimney. We should look elsewhere.

Of course if the fireplace was in the house when you purchased it, or if it was not built with attention to the principles of good fireplace construction, there may be several reasons why it smokes.

But there are remedies, and the chances that you can cure a smoky fireplace are all in your favor if you will apply diligence in locating and remedying the causes.

Whether the causes are due to construction or to other reasons, the ways of tracing the trouble are the same, and they should all be checked out carefully until the cause of the problem is located and corrected.

ENOUGH OXYGEN FOR THE FIRE?

This is where we should start looking. Is the fire smoking because it lacks enough air (oxygen) to allow for full combustion? Is the chimney stopped up with soot or a build-up of creosote? Did a bird build its nest in the chimney this summer?

And what about the damper? Is it open widely enough?

For fireplace operation, many houses are over-insulated, strange as it may seem. They have been so packed with insulating materials that there is scarcely any way for air to enter the house to feed the fire. You may notice, too, that you feel drowsy when the fire is burning; this could be from the same cause — a lack of oxygen.

Open the window slightly and see if this stops the smoking. If it does, then probably all you will need to do is to open a window in the basement or in some other distant room, and air will find its way to the fireplace.

If this is the cause of the smoke, you may prefer some other way to get adequate air to the fire rather than to open a house window. The artist who prepared the line drawings for this book incorporated a plan for this purpose into the construction of his home, and it works very successfully. He constructed an air passage from outside the house to the side of his fireplace. This may be opened as he pleases, and air is made available to the fire. There is no need to open any windows in the house to bring the fire more oxygen. The illustration shows how this was done.

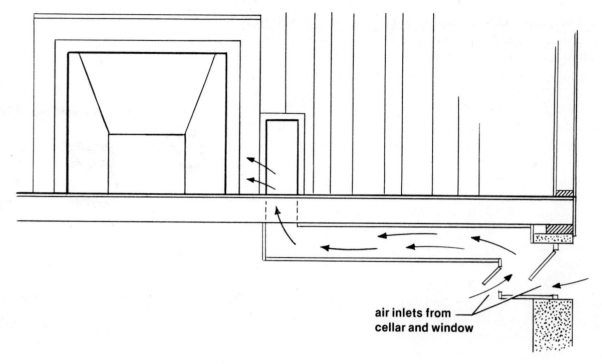

air inlets from —
cellar and window

From the above it is obvious that there are a number of ways this same solution could be handled. Furthermore, it is easily taken care of even if no provisions for it were made when the house was built. The local lumber yard or hardware store doubtless stocks four-inch flexible pipe that would make a connection from outside to the fireplace a simple project.

OUTSIDE DRAFTS AND BREEZES

"Smoky chimneys (fireplaces) in a new house are such, frequently, from mere want of air. . . . Those therefore who stop every crevice in a room to prevent the admission of fresh air, and yet would have their chimney carry up smoke, require inconsistencies, and expect impossibilities."

Benjamin Franklin,
On the Causes and Cure of Smoky Chimneys

So you tried more air and it doesn't stop the smoke? Let's go to the top of the chimney next and do a bit of investigating.

Check first to see that the spark arrester is not clogged with wet leaves on top, or with half burned paper on the underside.

Even though you built the chimney two feet above the ridge level and obeyed all the regulations in the building code, it just might be that the chimney is too short to provide an adequate draft. Try extending the length of the chimney flue. Probably the simplest way is to put another length of flue lining on top of the chimney (just temporarily) and see if that is the cure. Or you may pile up bricks to extend the flue. If you temporarily add on another three or four feet of flue and this does not stop the smoking, you should look for something else. But stay right there on the roof; we are not finished with the chimney yet.

Look around you. Are there other high buildings nearby, or tall trees that could deflect wind and breezes down toward the flue opening? This is a very common cause of smoky fireplaces, and it has nothing to do with the construction of the fireplace.

So what do we do?

Support a temporary hood about 10 inches over the top of the flue opening. The hood should be a little larger in area than the flue opening. This may stop the strong down-drafts caused by surrounding objects that are higher than your chimney top. But, if not, don't become discouraged.

If you have other flues in the same chimney, it could be that up-drafts from them are entering and descending the fireplace flue and are strong enough to prevent smoke from rising properly. Try closing these other flues with a piece of slate, for instance. If this stops the smoking problem, you should extend the length of the fireplace flue five or six inches above the others.

The cause of your problem may be a strong prevailing wind. In many parts of the country there are almost constant strong breezes that could become down-drafts in the fireplace flue. If you check a weathervane or flag, you will notice that these breezes almost always come from the same direction. If they come from the west, for example, build a ten-inch temporary extension to the chimney wall, being sure it is on the wind side (the west side in this case). See if it has stopped the smoking. If you have a chimney with two or more flues separated by a wythe, you might extend the wythe for the same reason, hoping it is perpendicular to the direction of the wind.

If this still is not the cure you are looking for, try building up two sides of the chimney for ten inches or so (perpendicular to the wind direction) and resting a hood on the top of them.

Should any of these temporary additions to the chimney and flue solve your problem, they should be taken down and replaced with permanent additions.

If your fireplace was built according to the Rumford principles, you should have located by this time the cause of the smoke from your fireplace. But, if not, we'll need to check the construction for any slip-ups when the fireplace was built.

If the fireplace was not built according to Rumford principles, you are more likely to find the cause of your trouble in the fire chamber. Let's take a look there.

A good thing about checking the fire chamber is that it is quite simple to make a few tests to see what may cause the smoke. Then when you locate the cause, a permanent correction can

CHECKING THE FIRE CHAMBER

be made, but the temporary checks do not cause any permanent damage to the fireplace.

We mentioned earlier that the relationship of the area of the flue liner opening to the area of the fire chamber opening is critical. One-tenth the area of the fire chamber is the recommended size for the area of the flue liner opening, but it should never be less than 1/12th the chamber opening.

Since it is impractical to enlarge the area of the chimney flue, if we think it is too small, let's reduce the area of the fireplace opening. Put a piece of sheet metal or even a board if you are just making a quick test, across the top of the fire chamber opening to reduce its size. Check it at various levels. Does this solve the smoke problem? If so, fashion a piece of steel, or perhaps copper, to replace the board and fasten it to the lintel, thus reducing the size of the fireplace opening. Another way would be to build a secondary lintel — inserting a new lintel into the brick jambs below the present lintel and at the same depth as the width of your testing board. The space between the two lintels should be filled with mortar or masonry. (A simple wood support wedged at the sides of the fire chamber under a framework directly under the new lintel will enable you to pour concrete between the two lintels or to support masonry while the space is being filled in.)

The wash is hung to dry in the Asa Slocumb House, built in 1790 in Shelburne and now part of the Shelburne (Vt.) Museum.

90

Another method of reducing the size of the fire chamber is to add another layer of firebricks to the back hearth. Try this first by placing them on top of the floor of the fire chamber. If this works, they can be cemented into place.

Is the width of the fireplace too great? According to Rumford it should be twice the depth of the fire chamber, but you should have no serious trouble if it is as much as three times; anything wider than that could cause trouble. (Both Count Rumford and Benjamin Franklin complained that fire chambers were frequently much too large, and better fires were found when the chambers were smaller.)

If you believe that your fireplace is too large, try bringing in the covings by piling up firebrick to make new ones, and thus reducing the width to a two or three times formula. It is a simple thing to build new covings if the width of the opening must be reduced.

A very common building mistake is to use the front edge of the damper for a lintel. This almost assures that there will be smoke in the room. We said earlier that the throat of the fireplace — that being the opening over which the damper is seated — should be eight to ten inches *above the lintel.* Otherwise the smoke following up the slope of the fireback will have no surface against which to turn and go up the chimney. The purpose of the breast is for just that — to deflect the smoke away from going into the room and instead to direct it up the chimney.

Possibly the same type hood mentioned above in connection with reducing the height of the fireplace opening could be installed to substitute for the breast. Or you could build another lintel as just mentioned. If this does not cure the problem and if you are sure this is where the problem is, you may need to tear down the brickwork, move the damper slightly toward the rear of the smoke shelf, and rebuild the fireback to line up with it.

But perhaps the trouble is with the fireback, especially if it is a continuous curve instead of a vertical rise from the hearth for approximately twelve inches and then an abrupt slant to the throat. This may require tearing out the present fireback and building another.

Did you check to see if the damper is too small? Remember that it should extend over the entire width of the fire chamber. What is the remedy for this one? Either tear it out and install a proper one, or else reduce the width of the fire chamber to conform to the length of the damper.

Is the throat too wide? It should never be more than four inches in width regardless of the size of the fireplace. Unless

Logs of elm trees killed by Dutch elm disease can be burned as firewood. These elm logs should be used the first winter or before the spring following the tree's death. This prevents the disease-carrying beetles from emerging and infecting healthy elms. If you can't burn all the dead elm wood, before spring, you should remove and burn the bark so that the larvae and eggs beneath this bark are destroyed."

USDA Leaflet 559,
Firewood for Your Fireplace

91

you can regulate this by closing the damper somewhat, it may be necessary to tear out some of the masonry and rebuild it to the proper width. This, too, may require a new fireback to bring it to the proper relationship with the opening of the throat.

It is hard to believe the mason forgot to build a smoke shelf, but perhaps he did. And if he did, you will almost certainly have to tear out a good portion of the fireback and make a smoke shelf; then rebuild the fireback. But possibly your fire chamber is deep enough so you can build a smoke shelf without tearing out the fireback — only remodeling it to provide for the smoke shelf.

Is the fire chamber too shallow? If so, lower the breast and design a smaller fire chamber.

CHECKING OUT THE FLUE

Occasionally we find that the flue is the culprit, and there are two common causes.

One is the installation of the flue liner when the flue is slanted for a certain distance. The liners must be cut and fitted in such a way that no jagged edges protrude to inhibit the continuous movement of drafts or to clog the flue with soot and other smoke wastes where they catch on the jagged edges. The remedy is to tear out the masonry and rebuild properly.

The other frequent cause is that the liners of two flues have been laid side-by-side, rather than offset, so their joints are directly opposite each other. Joints that are not perfectly tight can cause drafts from one flue to invade the other which causes a back-up of smoke. The correction of this is simple but requires careful workmanship to be certain that mortar does not fall down the flue and clog the smoke shelf and damper. Fill a bag with sand or dirt and fit it tightly inside the flue. Lower it with a rope to the joint levels; then pour thin mortar on the top of the bag and move the bag up and down so the mortar will flow into the open joints and seal them tightly.

More than one fire source using the same flue?

If so, this may very well be the cause of your trouble. One flue for each fire source is the rule. Occasionally someone will try to sneak another in just because the two fire sources are close together. Regardless of how small the second fire may be, it can cause great problems with the operation of your fireplace.

We hope you have found why your fireplace has been smoking and have been able to make permanent corrections to stop it. But if not, check with your local masonry supply houses for mechanical devices they sell to improve the up-drafts in the chimney. Some of these may work better than others, and only experience will determine whether they will help you. An interesting one we have seen recently, handcrafted on order for relatives who have smoke troubles, is a flue cap with slotted top that spins with the prevailing breeze, drawing air up the chimney. The owner reports complete success. In the event of strong winds or of too large a spinning top it is conceivable that this might draw warm air from the room up and out the chimney.

There is one device we would recommend — a patented log holder* made to keep the logs as close as possible to the rear of the fire chamber and high off the floor of the hearth. This is much more efficient than trying to maneuver andirons that are too long and too close to the hearth. Furthermore, since it raises the fire higher off the hearth than andirons do, it in effect shortens the height of the fire chamber in a much more simple and painless way than shortening it with a hood or installing a lower lintel.

MECHANICAL DEVICES

"By the help of this saving invention our wood may grow as fast as we consume it, and our posterity may warm themselves at a moderate rate, without being obliged to fetch their fuel over the Atlantic."

Benjamin Franklin,
writing about the Pennsylvanian Fireplace he invented.

* Available from Garden Way Living Center, Williston Road, South Burlington, Vermont 05401

10 Wood and Other Fuels

Even the best fireplace will not produce a good fire unless the fire is properly laid and the right fuel is used.

When we think of fireplace fuel, we usually think of wood. And in those areas where wood is expensive and gas is used instead, even the gas is frequently fed through imitation logs. Yes, fireplaces and wood just seem to go together.

Wood has a lot going for it. It is a renewable natural resource which is easier and, in most cases, cheaper, to obtain than fossil fuels. Even trees which are undesirable for other purposes — those that are deformed, diseased, and genetically poor — can be culled and used for firewood, giving the good trees more room in which to develop as timber or pulpwood.

Wood also ignites quickly when dry and gives a hot flame, and its ash, usually only 1 percent, can be used for fertilizer. Furthermore, wood does not add to air pollution since the products released by burning would be released eventually by decay, albeit more slowly.

There are a few disadvantages to its use as a fuel. Not only does it have to be cut and seasoned, but wood has to be stored; and this may require a large storage space or shed. And it almost always has to be transported some distance from where it is cut to where it will be burned. These disadvantages make it rather impractical for the city dweller to use wood except for an occasional fire.

WHERE TO GET WOOD

Where would you get wood if you wanted it?

If you have no forested land or your own to cut, you might try the local dump. You may be surprised at the amount of wood that is thrown into dumps and landfills where burning is forbidden. Power companies often have limbs and tops from their maintenance work which are available for the taking. Some national forests allow the cutting of firewood; and a phone call to the local district ranger of your forest service will advise if you may cut wood there. Check state, county, and city forests as well. In recent years with so much concern about the energy crunch, a number of the state forests have measured off sections where one may cut wood for free or for a token fee. The land is then replanted with young trees.

A truck will almost certainly be needed to haul the wood home. Give some thought about how you are going to get your wood supply home if you do the cutting yourself.

HOW TO BUY WOOD

If you can find wood in no other way, you can always check the "for sale" notices in the local paper and order what you need, in which case you will doubtless want to specify that it be delivered.

Wood is usually sold by the *cord*. But don't be misled. There is a difference in cords — they are not all alike.

A standard cord is a stack of logs which measures four feet high by eight feet long and four feet deep, or its equivalent. This contains 128 cubic feet. Sometimes, however, a cord is not a standard cord but instead a *face cord*. A face cord is a stack four feet high, eight feet long, but the depth is only the length of the logs — 12, 16 or 24 inches. It will therefore contain far fewer cubic feet that a standard cord. A face cord may also be called a *short cord,* or a *rack,* or a *rick*.

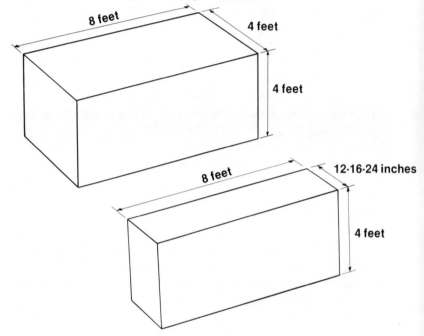

Other kinds of cords you may encounter could be a "stove cord," a "fireplace cord," or a "pick-up cord" — all less than a standard cord but labeled in a way that confuses or misleads the buyer. Be certain you know exactly what kind of cord you are buying, else you may be paying far too much for the amount you will get, and getting far less than you really need.

There is no way to pack wood logs so tightly that there is no waste space between them. It is estimated that a standard cord contains not 128 cubic feet of wood, but about ninety. The volume of solid wood depends on the care in piling, thickness of the logs, and whether they are round or split. Bark thickness and bent logs can further shrink the actual number of cubic feet.

Sometimes wood is sold by the ton. Wood shrinks as it dries, so a cord of green wood (newly cut wood) loses weight when it dries. If you are buying green or wet wood, let the seller heap two or three more inches on the pile to allow for shrinkage; otherwise you will be paying for water instead of fuel.

Also, if you are buying cut wood, try to get logs that will fit your fireplace, not so long that you will have to cut them again after the wood is delivered. Thick logs should be split because split wood ignites more quickly and burns better than round logs that have less surface for easy firing. A mixture of split and round logs as well as a variety of hardwoods is usually most satisfactory.

WHAT IS BEST FOR BURNING?

First, it should be dry and well seasoned. Wet wood does not lower the fuel value, but it does reduce the overall heating efficiency since the cooling effect of the water prevents complete combustion. Wet wood ignites more slowly, it will go out more quickly, and it is more likely to smoke. A build-up of creosote in the fireplace and chimney is often a result of burning green wood, and creosote contributes to fire hazards. If you must burn green wood, put it on a fire that is already hot and burning well. Keep in mind that a log of green ash has a relatively low moisture content and burns better than most green woods.

The best fires — those most satisfactory from the point of view of care, burning efficiency, and heat — are made from hardwoods: oak, hickory, maple, iron wood, white or yellow birch, beech, walnut, and ash. Fruitwoods such as cherry and apple are also very good. Elm trees that have died of the Dutch elm disease can be cut up for firewood. If the dead tree is left with the bark on, it will harbor the beetles that transmit the disease. If the bark is stripped and burned, the elm will no longer be a source of trouble. Beech burns with a steady flame. Apple and hickory add a pleasant aroma.

Some of the softer hardwoods do not burn as long although they ignite more quickly. These include aspen, willow, cottonwood, poplar, and basswood. White birch, although more dense than these, also seems to burn more quickly. Driftwood from the sea, because of the salt it has absorbed, burns with various colors.

Softwoods burn with a quick hot flame, but because they do not last very long, they are not a good source of heat. They make excellent kindling. In general, softwoods are those that do not shed their leaves (needles) and include pine, fir, hemlock, and spruce. They also tend to shoot off sparks which start fires in the room, and the resin in the wood may leave a

"Firewood may be available from the National Forests. Check with your nearest Forest Service District Ranger for more detailed information. State Foresters, county Extension Agents, and county and city foresters can also provide information on local sources of firewood."

USDA Leaflet 559,
Firewood for Your Fireplace

residue in the chimney to cause chimney fires if allowed to build up.

In the West, preferred hardwoods are manzanite, eucalyptus, madrone, red alder and tan oak. Softwoods are pine, Douglas fir, spruce, and redwood. Southwest species most popular are oak (Gambel, Arizona white and Arizona live), alligator juniper, Utah juniper, one-seed juniper, and ponderosa pine. In the Northwest the most popular are red alder and Douglas fir with red cedar for kindling.

In the Texas area the largest percentage of wood used is red oak (southern red, black, shumard, willow and water), white oak (Burr, post, swamp chestnut) or ash (green or white). Some other woods are red maple, American beech, river birch, elm, hickory, hackberry, sycamore, sweetgum, and black willow. Southern pine burns too fast to be of much use.

WOOD
SUBSTITUTES

Beechwood fires are bright and clear
If the logs are kept a year.
Chestnut only good, they say,
If for long 'tis laid away.
But ash new or ash old
Is fit for queen with crown of gold.

Birch and fir logs burn too fast,
Blaze up bright and do not last.
It is by the Irish said
Hawthorn bakes the sweetest bread.
Elm wood burns like churchyard mold,
E'en the very flames are cold.
But ash green or ash brown
Is fit for queen with golden crown.

Poplar gives a bitter smoke,
Fills your eyes and makes you choke.
Apple wood will scent your room
With an incense like perfume.
Oaken logs, if dry and old,
Keep away the winter's cold.
But ash wet or ash dry
A king shall warm his slippers by.

Anonymous English Poet

Pressed wood logs are commonly used and are made from sawdust put together under great pressure. Sometimes a glue or resin binder is used. These are clean, easy to store and handle, have little smoke and low ash, and give off more heat per pound than do wooden logs. They are much more expensive than wood, but they may be the only available fuel for those who live too far from a wood supply, or who do not have a place to store wood. Sometimes these artificial logs are treated chemically to burn with colored flames. Pressed logs, about 18 inches long, are usually sold in boxes or bundles of four or six logs at lumber yards, hardware stores, and, yes, even at the supermarket.

Charcoal and charcoal briquettes make a quick, hot flame with little or no odor, but they must be burned in a room with plenty of ventilation inasmuch as charcoal that is incompletely burned gives off carbon monoxide, a poisonous gas.

Coal may be burned in the fireplace. After being kindled with wood, it burns slowly with a steady flame and heats well. Like charcoal, it is not as pretty to look at as is a wood fire. Furthermore, a special grate is required to keep the coal off the floor of the hearth. Cannel coal, a soft coal, is satisfactory fuel, but one should use a screen to prevent its sparks from flying outside the fireplace. Also, cannel coal is quite likely to deposit soot in the chimney, which, if ignited, would cause a chimney fire. It is sometimes all packaged for sale ready for the fireplace and a touch of the match.

Where other fuels are not available, gas may be used. It is

convenient and can be made to look somewhat realistic when piped through imitation logs. Little heat is given off. Special piping is required to bring gas into the hearth area. If city gas is not available, butane tanks can be used. See your gas dealer on how best to connect it.

Newspapers are another source of fuel for those who find wood impractical. They first must be made into "logs" to insure long, even burning. To make these logs, stack a pile of newspapers a half-inch high. The width of the pile should be the length you propose for your log. Soak this pile overnight in a bathtub or laundry tub of water to which a tablespoon of detergent has been added. The next day, roll the pile around a broomstick, squeezing and compressing it with your fingers to break down the fibers. Fasten the ends with tape or rubber bands, withdraw the broomstick, and stand the roll ("log") on end to dry. In one to three weeks your log should be dry enough for burning. It should burn for several hours.

The logs can be made with paste instead of water. Coat the broomstick with oil, brush library paste on the top sheet of paper, roll it around the broomstick and continue rolling each sheet from the pile, first brushing with paste. When the log is thick enough, fasten its ends with rubber bands or tape, then slip it off the broomstick to dry.

It is also possible to buy gadgets for rolling the newspapers. Newspaper logs burn very well and provide free fuel for those who read the dailies.

"Generally speaking, a standard cord of air dry, dense hardwood weighs approximately two tons and provides as much heat as one ton of coal, or 150-175 gallons of No. 2 fuel oil, or 24,000 cubic feet of natural gas."

USDA Leaflet 559,
Firewood for Your Fireplace

SEASONING AND STORING WOOD

Green or freshly cut wood should be seasoned before being used, and attempts to get moisture out of wood should begin as soon as it is cut to prevent decay. Air is the most important factor; therefore, wood should be piled loosely to allow as much air as possible to surround it. Splitting wood will also hasten drying because it will increase the amount of surface exposed to the air. While wood cut in the spring may be used the following winter, it is even better to dry wood outside during the first summer and winter and inside under cover the next summer. This usually means about nine to twelve months of drying outdoors if you live in the North. Six months in the South is probably adequate. Another six months or so of drying under cover is also necessary.

Until it is brought into the house, the wood should be stored under a roof, or it may be covered with heavy plastic held down with logs or stones. Firewood should never be stored directly on the ground or it will rot. Raise it off the ground with flat stones or scrap wood.

Split wood not only dries faster, but it also burns better; so be sure to have plenty of split wood on hand. Green wood is easier to split than dry wood, and wood is easier to split when it is frozen. Split the logs that are straight-grained and with few knots to make the job easier. There are several woods that have a reputation as being difficult to split: elm, black gum, grey birch, and rock maple, for example. Better burn them whole unless you want the exercise. And don't forget that a blunt axe is better for splitting than a sharp one. For the real hard-to-split pieces wedges and a sledge hammer may be required.

An attractive woodbox near the fireplace is a good place to keep wood ready for use. Sometimes the fireplace may be built with cabinets alongside, with or without doors for this purpose. Sometimes, too, a cabinet may have a door at the back, opening into the garage or the outside. This makes it possible to fill the woodbox without carrying wood through the room. Those with upstairs fireplaces may want to consider building a dumbwaiter that can raise the firewood from below.

To guard against ants, beetles, and other insects that live in wood from coming out into your living room, store only a day's supply of wood at a time near the fireplace.

"They warmed me twice, — once while I was splitting them, and again when they were on the fire, so that no fuel could give out more heat."

Henry D. Thoreau,
Walden

HOW TO
BUILD THE FIRE

Wood burns in three stages. First the wood dries out, then combustible and non-combustible gases are released, and finally the solid carbonized material burns. Nitrogen and carbon dioxide (the non-combustible gases) go into the atmosphere; carbon monoxide, hydrogen and methane (the combustible gases) will burn completely, leaving only ashes, providing there is enough oxygen to feed the fire.

There are several factors that affect the combustion. These are the amount of moisture in the wood, the moisture formed by the burning hydrogen, the amount of air available for combustion, the heat carried away with chimney gases, unconsumed solid matter, and the radiation losses from the fireplace chamber where fuel is consumed.

It is good to have one or two inches of ashes in the hearth. This will keep the heat in the coals and can be used to bank the fire overnight. Since it is important that air circulate around the firewood, andirons, a grate, an iron basket, or even a few bricks to raise it off the hearth will prove very useful.

Place some crumpled newspaper under the grate or andirons;

then add tinder or small kindling on top of the paper. Next, lay two logs on the andirons, one close to the fireback and the other near the front of the andirons or grate. Some kindling should be placed on top of these two logs and a third log over the kindling. It is important to have at least three logs since they feed heat to each other and will keep the fire burning, whereas one log will go out because it alone does not generate enough heat to maintain the fire.

Before you strike the match, DON'T FORGET TO OPEN THE DAMPER. There is no place for the smoke to go but into the room if the damper is closed.

And that is not all. If the fireplace has not been used for a few hours, there is a very good possibility there is a down-draft in the flue that will prevent smoke from rising. What to do? Twist or roll some newspaper into a torch, light it, and hold it high up under the damper until its heat turns the down-draft around and you notice that the flames seem to be pulled up the flue. Now you are ready to light the newspaper under the fire you have laid, and you should not experience any smoke problem.

Another method of building a fire is to put down crumpled paper and tinder, and then pile kindling and logs in tepee fashion.

"Better a wee fire to warm ye
Than a big fire to burn ye."

Scotch proverb

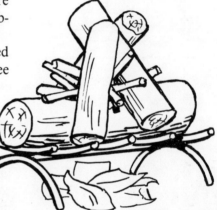

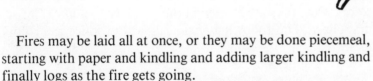

Fires may be laid all at once, or they may be done piecemeal, starting with paper and kindling and adding larger kindling and finally logs as the fire gets going.

Keep the fire as close to the fireback as possible. This not only makes it easier for the smoke to go up the chimney but it also radiates more heat into the room.

If logs are still burning when you wish to extinguish the fire, stand them on end against the fireback, and the fire will go out quickly. The partially burned logs will be ready for burning in your next fire.

Should you be burning coal, pieces of coal may be added with tongs after the kindling fire has been well established. Be sure to have adequate ventilation so there will be complete combustion of the carbon monoxide that will be released.

After you become expert at fire building, experiment a bit with raising and lowering the damper. You will find you are

able to control the amount of fire you prefer. When the fire dies down to coals, the damper can be almost closed to prevent heat in the room from escaping up the chimney. But be sure to open it wide again before building the next fire.

There are several devices on the market that make it easier to ignite the fire. One is the common Cape Cod lighter. This is a metal container of kerosene and a metal handle attached to a ball of soapstone or other porous non-inflammable material which is kept submerged in the kerosene. When the ball is removed from the container and lighted, the kerosene that has been absorbed will burn for quite some time, certainly long enough to ignite the kindling. The lighter may be left in the fire until its flame is spent, then removed to cool before it is returned to the container.

Electric lighters are also available, usually from hardware stores, where you may also find gas lighters.

Many people prefer colored flames, and a common item in hardware stores and supermarkets is canned powder to be sprinkled on the fire to produce color. If you wish to save money, make the powder yourself from chemicals you may purchase from the local drugstore.

The U.S. Department of Agriculture has issued some guidelines for the homeowner who wishes to produce colored flames in his fireplace:

Evergreen cones, small blocks of wood or kindling, wood chips and sawdust, or even one-inch diameter rolls of tightly wrapped newspapers or magazines tied at both ends, soaked in chemical solutions and dried will give off flames of various colors when they are burned in the fireplace to add to Christmas cheer. The following chemicals will produce the colors indicated:

1. Copper sulfate .... green
2. Calcium chloride .... orange
3. Copper chloride .... blue
4. Lithium chloride................ carmine
5. Potassium chloride.............. purple

DO NOT USE CHLORATES OR NITRATES, OR POTASSIUM PERMANGANATE. Chemicals should be kept away from children and pets. To avoid storage, obtain only sufficient amounts for treatment. This job should be done outdoors.

Rubber gloves should be worn and care used not to spill the chemicals or solutions. The chemicals should be dissolved in a **wooden pail** or earthen crock, since the chemicals will ultimately destroy metal containers. A discarded five-gallon paint bucket serves admirably as a treating vat, mixing in it no more than a couple gallons of solution at a time. No need to cleanse it thoroughly for a change of chemicals. The ratio is one pound of chemical to one gallon of water, using one chemical per batch.

The materials to be treated may be placed in a mesh or porous bag, and submerged in the solution. A stone can weigh the material down in the solution. A day or so of soaking should be adequate. Lift out and drain over the container and spread the treated materials to dry. If the materials are allowed to dry on newspapers, the newspapers themselves, when dry, may be rolled and tied tightly to burn in the fireplace.

The burning of treated materials should be confined to a well-ventilated fireplace.

There are several tools which are handy around a fireplace. They save a lot of time and keep one from being burned while moving hot logs. It is a good investment to buy a pair of tongs and a poker, and a brush is handy for cleaning the hearth. A small shovel will assist in removing ashes, and a bellows is useful to persuade a reluctant flame.

Any fire can be dangerous, and an open fire is especially so. For that reason there are several precautions that should be taken.

Here's a list of the most important ones:

SAFETY PRECAUTIONS

1. Always be sure the damper is open and the downdrafts have been turned back before lighting a fire.

2. A fire screen will stop sparks from shooting into the room. Every fireplace should have a screen.

3. The front hearth should extend at least twenty inches in front of the fireplace opening and be made of fireproof material.

4. Rugs and floor coverings close to the fireplace should be made of fire-resistant material.

5. Except for kerosene in a Cape Cod lighter, do not use petrochemicals to start a fire.

6. Do not burn household trash in the fireplace. This is especially dangerous with plastics, many of which give off toxic fumes when burned.

7. Be sure there is plenty of oxygen to feed the fire. This may require opening a window a bit, but plenty of air is needed to assure that combustible gases are consumed.

8. Do not use fans in the house when there is a fire in the fireplace. Fans frequently set up a new draft pattern that pulls the fire outside of the fire chamber into the room, bringing with it smoke and gases. Fans will even suck ashes through a fire screen into the room. Fans used in conjunction with forced-air heating are as much the culprit as any other fan.

9. Don't burn green, wet, resinous woods as they may coat the flue with tar and increase the danger of chimney fire. Hemlock, larch, spruce, and juniper give off sparks and should be used with caution.

RATINGS FOR FIREWOOD

Hardwood trees	Relative amt. of heat	Easy to burn	Easy to split	Heavy smoke?	Pop or throw sparks?	General rating and remarks
Ash, red oak, beech, birch, hickory, hard maple, pecan, dogwood	High	Yes	Yes	No	No	Excellent
Soft maple, cherry, walnut	Medium	Yes	Yes	No	No	Good
Elm, sycamore, gum	Medium	Medium	No	Medium	No	Fair—contains too much water when green
Aspen, basswood, cottonwood, yellow poplar	Low	Yes	Yes	Medium	No	Fair—but good for kindling
Softwood trees						
Southern yellow pine, Douglas fir	High	Yes	Yes	Yes	No	Good but smoky
Cypress, redwood	Medium	Medium	Yes	Medium	No	Fair
White cedar, western red cedar, eastern red cedar	Medium	Yes	Yes	Medium	Yes	Good—excellent for kindling
Eastern white pine, western white pine, ponderosa pine, true firs	Low	Medium	Yes	Medium	No	Fair—good kindling
Tamarack, larch	Medium	Yes	Yes	Medium	Yes	Fair
Spruce	Low	Yes	Yes	Medium	Yes	Poor—but good for kindling

From: U.S. Department of Agriculture, Forest Service, Leaflet No. 559, Issued 1974

11 Maintenance and Use

Like the rest of the house, the chimney and fireplace need periodic maintenance and preventive care.

The chimney should be inspected each fall. It may need cleaning and repairing. The place to start is on the roof. Lower a light on an extension cord into the chimney and look inside. Check for loose or fallen bricks, cracks, and breaks in the flue lining, and clogged flue liners. Did the birds raise their young in the chimney during the summer? Check to see how much soot has accumulated. On the outside of the chimney prod the mortar joints with a knife to check for loose bricks and joints. Also look for weathering bricks and mortar. Notice the flashing around the chimney to be sure it is still shedding moisture and not leaking.

To inspect the chimney for cracks, build a small fire in the hearth and put a wet blanket or newspaper on top of the chimney. Then sniff for and try to find smoke escaping through the chimney walls. Any sign of escaping smoke indicates a crack in the chimney or loose mortar that needs repair.

Sometime when there is a fire burning, go over the entire chimney indoors and out to feel with your hand for hot places. If any place is too hot for your hand, it is too hot for your house. You should call in a professional for advice, and a good person to call would be the fire chief or an experienced mason.

If a build-up of soot is noticed, the easiest way to get rid of it is to call in a professional company to vacuum it. Such businesses have the equipment and can perform the task quickly and with little or no dirt and fuss. But if there is no such business in your area, or if you wish to avoid the expense, there are things you can do yourself.

First close off the fireplace opening to keep soot from spreading all over the room and the furniture. Seal it with tape. Then go back up on the roof. At the end of a long rope or wire, attach a weighted sack filled with hay, straw, or even with tire chains. Work the sack up and down inside the chimney to loosen the soot. A small evergreen tree such as a Christmas tree will also do the trick. So will loose tire chains.

Once the soot has been loosened and dropped to the bottom, remove it through the fireplace opening. Reach well up into the smoke chamber and clean it all out. Be sure none of it remains piled up on the smoke shelf or on the damper.

Check also for a build-up of creosote, the gummy or often hard residue left by imperfect combustion that could have been caused by burning green wood or resinous wood, the vapors of which condensed and adhered to a cool chimney. This is not so easy to remove, so it is best to avoid the risk of accumulating it in the first place by burning the proper kind of wood. Creosote can be extremely dangerous once it catches fire. The force of the flames trying to find an outlet can cause cracks and even explosions in the chimney.

The best way to remove creosote is to scrape it off with a sharp blade or with a long-handled hoe. Sometimes heavy tire chains will also remove it. Care should be taken not to fracture the flue liner or flue joints. The creosote, too, will have to be removed through the fire chamber.

"If you are cleaning a fireplace chimney, a fine way is to scour it with a small birch tree, or the upper limbs of a larger birch tree. One person standing on the roof and another in front of the fireplace, can haul the tree back and forth on ropes. A birch tree has stout, spiky limbs, like a big wire brush."

OEO Pamphlet 6143-5,
Save Energy: Save Money

106

We strongly urge that, unless creosote can be removed easily, a professional chimney-cleaning crew be hired to do this. Such crews are experienced and have the proper tools for the job. Their fee may be a great deal less than repair bills if damage is done by an inexperienced homeowner with make-shift tools.

Chemicals are sometimes used to clean the chimney and remove creosote. They are not recommended, however, since they usually are not too effective, and sparks may later ignite chemical residues and any remaining creosote.

Small amounts of chemicals may be put on the fire once a week to control the build-up of soot and creosote. Such chemicals are sold in hardware stores, sometimes available in decorated containers. But you can save money if you make your own chemical mixtures.

The cheapest, most available, and easiest to handle although not the most effective, is rock salt. Metallic zinc dust or small granules of it are quite effective. Or try a mixture of two parts rock salt and one part pulverized zinc. Rock salt plus 10 percent zinc dust by volume is more effective than either the salt or zinc alone. Another recipe calls for one cup of household salt and one cup of zinc oxide powder. Still another calls for one part dry lead and five parts household salt (parts by weight) mixed together. Calcium chloride or a combination of household salt and copper sulfate are also suggested. All these chemicals should be used in powder or crystalline form, and they should be handled with care. Be sure to wash your hands after handling them, especially if you use lead, which is poisonous. Mix whatever combination you choose in a can and sprinkle a cup or two on a hot fire or over coals once a week. If your druggist does not have these chemicals, he will know where you may obtain them.

Should your inspection of the chimney reveal cracks or loose joints, they must be repaired. Cracks inside the flue may be repaired outside the chimney from the roof. Lower a weighted canvas bag into the chimney. Be sure it fits tightly enough so a good tug is required to pull it back up. Lower it to just below the crack that is to be repaired. Pour grout (a thin mortar mix) on top of the bag, and, moving the bag up and down, work the grout into the crack and seal it. Then move on to the next place to be repaired. You will find that a slightly liquid consistency of grout will work into the crack better than a stiff mixture.

Loose mortar joints on the outside of the chimney will also need repair. Pry out the loose mortar with a knife and dampen the open joint before forcing new mortar into it. Dampening

"Chimneys should be inspected every fall for defects. Check for loose or fallen bricks, cracked or broken flue lining, and excessive soot accumulation by lowering an electric light into the flue. Mortar joints can be tested from the outside by prodding with a knife."

USDA Farmers' Bulletin 1889

"If soot stains the facing of your fireplace, try scrubbing it off with strong detergent and water. If this doesn't work, use a mild acetic acid diluted with water. For really stubborn stains, scrub with a solution of muriatic acid (one part acid with ten parts water) and rinse off immediately. Warning: Use rubber gloves with any acid. Other methods you might try: coarse steel wool or a steel-bristled brush and an abrasive compound such as mechanic's hand cleaner or a paste of carborundum and water."

Doug Merrilees,
Curing Smoky Fireplaces

will prevent the dry brick from absorbing all the moisture in the mortar and will allow the new mortar to dry slowly to make a bond. Mortar made of two parts clean sand and one part portland cement will be fine for the work. If you can't find any portland cement, use roofing cement or even mastic, but get the joint repaired. Use your pointing trowel to match the finish of the new mortar to the old. It is also a good idea to coat the outside of the chimney with a colorless masonry sealer.

If the fire chamber joints should be repaired and repointed, or loose bricks replaced, use commercial fire clay or a strong concrete mixture.

If the facing of the fireplace is stained by soot or smoke, it can be cleaned although it is sometimes a bit difficult. For simple stains, scrubbing with a brush using strong soap and water may be sufficient. Or scrub with a mild acid bleach — a vinegar or acetic acid solution. Scrubbing with a solution of one tablespoon of tri-sodium phosphate in a gallon of water also is good for mild stains. Then rinse the brick with clear water and dry it with a cloth. For stains on smooth bricks, rubbing with a carborundum rod or block (such as used for sharpening knives) may remove them. For common brick, scrub with coarse steel wool and water and a grit-containing mechanic's hand-cleaning compound. The color of the brick can be restored by painting with raw linseed oil.

If the stains refuse to budge, something stronger will be required. Put on your rubber gloves and work carefully. Mix one part hydrochloric acid (also sold under the name of muriatic acid) in a glass jar with ten parts of water. Apply this to the stain with a rag. Rinse immediately. This mixture also will remove construction stains. Since the mixture will discolor some types of bricks, it is best to test first on a piece of scrap brick. Do not use this on stonework.

Another method is to mix six ounces of oxalic acid crystals in a quart of warm water, adding enough lime or whiting to form a soft paste. Spread it on the stains with a broad knife or spatula and leave for fifteen minutes. Rinse and dry. Oxalic acid is a poison. Be very careful using it.

Hearth tiles and flagstones are best cleaned with warm, soapy water, then rinsed and dried. Liquid floor wax applied to dry tiles and flagstones gives them a good finish and provides some protection against stains. So does boiled linseed oil, the excess of which should be wiped off after about thirty minutes.

Proper periodic repair and cleaning of the chimney and the burning of dry wood should eliminate the risks of chimney fires. But should one occur, the first thing to do is to call the

108

fire department. Until firemen arrive, throw salt or baking powder on the fire to extinguish it in the hearth. Wet down your roof with a garden hose.

Even though the fire is in the flue, the fire in the hearth should be extinguished first. Then a wet blanket or rug should be placed over the fireplace opening to shut off air to the fire. Close doors to other rooms to prevent smoke and soot damage. If the chimney was built with flue liners, the chances of fire damage to the house will be greatly reduced. By all means, take care to protect yourself and family in the event of fire. Let the fire department take over as soon as it arrives.

Unusual use of brick is noted in this fireplace, one of six in the Stencil House, built around 1790 in Columbus, N.Y., and now in the Shelburne (Vt.) Museum.

Hagar House —1818

This home of Donald Ballou in Middlebury, Vermont, has a center chimney in excellent proportion to the rest of the house, and not hinting at the immense size of fireplace construction beneath it.

Three fireplaces in the house include this one in the dining room, with its satisfying lines and its white Vermont marble mantel framed in a gleaming white wood paneling. Home was built in 1818 by Jonathan Hagar, and features three fireplaces, all with Vermont marble mantels of conservative lines.

Fixtures in shiny brass contrast with the white marble and paneling of the living room fireplace. Behind this and the other two first-floor fireplaces is a spacious ham smoking room.

The sturdy base of the Hagar home fireplace dominates the cellar, measuring fourteen feet, three inches, by ten feet, nine inches. That base contains four brick-arched rooms like the one at left. Fitted with shelves, and not warmed by the fires above them, they provide excellent storage space for wine and canned foods.

The largest of the three fireplaces is the kitchen fireplace pictured below. It's a fireplace built for cooking and heating, and features a huge, deep oven, at right, as well as a sturdy iron double pot holder. The owner has retained the practical flavor of the past by equipping it and the mantel with the tools and equipment a family would have used generations ago.

Imaginative Ideas

In a huge room, this stone fireplace serves as a gathering place, and two comfortable sofas further create this image of warmth and friendliness.

These two photographs show a handy feature of the fireplace, which is a wood storage space built into the stonework. Photo at right is of outside door, permitting loading of wood directly into the storage space, without tracking through the room.

These Brick Institute of America photographs hint at the variety of imaginative fireplaces possible. From upper left and clockwise they include a muted background for oriental decor; a hood to permit construction of a "fire shelf" and indoor barbecue grill; a soaring brick wall that doubles as a fireplace and a fire-sound barrier, and a cooking center in the kitchen, as functional as it is beautiful.

The kettle hangs, ready for making tea, in this fireplace in the Dutton House, built in Cavendish, Vt., in 1782, and now a part of the Shelburne (Vt.) Museum. In photo below, from Brick Institute of America, a skylight at the peak of this cathedral ceiling casts sunlight on a pattern sculptured in brick.

Fireplaces in photos above and below are in homes where comfort and informal living are stressed. Top fireplace offers opportunity for cooking. (Brick Institute of America)

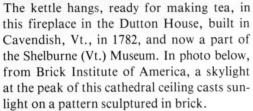

Outdoors
or Indoors

A formal air is added to this living room by this fireplace (Portland Willamette Co.).Lower photo, from Brick Institute of America, shows effective use of raised hearth, linking fireplace with window at left.

107"   8.9'
50"   4.2'

A deck overlooking the waterfront, an outdoor fireplace for gracious entertaining, that's easy living. (Brick Institute of America)

Sources of Information

WHERE CAN I GET IT?

The following list includes a few of the places to obtain supplies and information. It is by no means a complete list.

Chemicals for cleaning fireplace exteriors and chimneys

Drug stores   Lumber companies
Hardware stores   Mail order catalogs

Chimneys, including caps, flues, dampers and damper controls, fans, clean-outs, grills and brick vents

Chim-a-lator   Quick Draft Corporation
8824 Wentworth Ave. South   1525 Perry Drive, S.W.
Minneapolis, MN 55420   P.O. Box 1353, Station C
                                Canton, OH 44708

The Majestic Company   Vega Industries
Huntington, IN 44650   Syracuse, NY 13205

National Sewer Pipe Limited   Vestal Manufacturing Co.
P.O. Box 1800   Box 420
Oakville, Ontario, Canada   Sweetwater, TN 37874

Fireplace accessories including grates, screens, log carriers, pokers, andirons, baskets, etc.

Bennett-Ireland   Frank Fusco
23 State St.   56 Upland Dr.
Norwich, CT 13815   East Northport, NY 11731

Canterbury Enterprises   Garden Way Research
6253 Hollywood Blvd.   Charlotte, VT 05445
Los Angeles, CA 90028

Hearth Shoppe Products Co.
P.O. Box 11
Oreland, PA 19705

Loeffler Heating Units
    Mfg. Co.
R.D. 1 Box 503
Branchville, NJ 07826

The Majestic Company
Huntington, IN 46750

Operators Heat, Inc.
1601 W. 41 St.
Baltimore, MD 21211

Portland Willamette Co.
6802 N.E. 59th Place
Portland, OR 97218

Radiant Grate, Inc.
Emil and Alethea Dahlquist
31 Morgan Park
Clinton, CT 06413

Royal-DeSoto
Judd Road
Chattanooga, TN 37406

Seymour Manufacturing Co.
Seymour, IN 47274

Superior Fireplace Co.
4325 Artesia Ave.
Fullerton, CA 92633

Tamro Industries, Inc.
2347 28th St. S.E.
Grand Rapids, MI 49506

Thermograte
51 Iona Lane
St. Paul, MN 55117

Thermo-Rite Mfg. Co.
Box 1108
Akron, OH 44309

Vestal Manufacturing Co.
Box 420
Sweetwater, TN 37874

Virginia Metal Crafters
1101 E. Main St.
Waynesboro, VA 22980

Mail order catalogs and department stores usually carry fireplace accessories.

Free-standing Fireplaces

Condon-King Co.
5611 208th Ave. S.W.
Lynnwood, WA 98063

Fasco Industries, Inc.
255 N. Union St.
Rochester, NY 14605

Heatilator
Vega Industries Inc.
Mt. Pleasant, IA 53641

Kristia Associates
P.O. Box 1461
Portland, ME 04104

Lincoln Steel Corp.
Box 1668
Lincoln, NE 68501

The Majestic Company
Huntington, IN 46750

Malm Fireplaces, Inc.
368 Yolanda Ave.
Santa Rosa, CA 95404

Northwest Tube and
   and Metal Fabricators
P.O. Box 02214
Portland, OR 97202

Preway, Inc.
Wisconsin Rapids, WI 54494

Rangaire Corp.
P.O. Box 177
Cleburne, TX 76031

Readybuilt Products Co.
1701 McHenry St.
Baltimore, MD 21223

Robert H. Peterson Co.
2835 Sierra Grande St.
Pasadena, CA 91107

Royal-DeSoto
Judd Road
Chattanooga, TN 37406

Superior Fireplace Co.
4325 Artesia Ave.
Fullerton, CA 92633

Temco Inc.
4101 Charlotte Ave.
Nashville, TN 37202

Thermo-Rite Mfg. Co.
Box 1108
Akron, OH 44309

United States Stove Co.
South Pittsburg, TN 47480

Washington Stove Works
Box 687
Everett, WA 98206

Many mail order firms carry a good assortment of free-standing fireplaces.

Franklin Stoves

Atlanta Stove Works, Inc.
P.O. Box 5254
Atlanta, GA 30307

Kristia Associates
P.O. Box 1461
Portland, ME 04104

Portland Stove Foundry Co.
57 Kennebec Street
Portland, ME 04104

United States Stove Co.
South Pittsburg, TN 37380

Washington Stove Works
P.O. Box 687
Everett, WA 98201

Literature

Books and leaflets are available from the following:
U.S. Department of Agriculture, Washington, D.C.
State Universities, especially the Colleges of Agriculture
State University Extension Services

Magazines frequently carry articles on some aspects of fireplaces and fire-building. Some magazines in which you might expect to find such articles are:
House and Garden
Better Homes and Gardens
Changing Times
Books. The following are just a few of the useful books on wood, fireplaces, and fire building:

Clegg, Peter. *Energy for the Home.* Garden Way Publishing Co., Charlotte, VT 05445

Gay, Larry. *The Complete Book of Heating With Wood.* Garden Way Publishing Co., Charlotte, VT 05445

Lytle, R. J. and Marie-Jeanne. *Book of Successful Fireplaces.* Structures Publishing Co., Farmington, MI 48024

Orton, Vrest. *The Forgotten Art of Building a Good Fireplace,* Yankee, Dublin, NH 03444

Rowsome, Frank, Jr. *A Bright And Glowing Place.* Stephen Greene Press, Brattleboro, VT 05301

Sunset House. *How to Plan and Build Your Fireplace.* Sunset House, Menlo Park CA 94025

Mantels

The Endeavor Periods, Inc.
1485 Berger Dr.
San Jose, CA 95112

Readybuilt Products Co.
1701 McHenry St.
Baltimore, MD 21223

Masons

Yellow pages of your local phone book
Local builders

Modified fireplaces

American Stovalator Corp.
Box 435
Ten Seminary Place
Manchester, VT 05254

Heatilator
Vega Industries, Inc.
Mt. Pleasant, IA 52641

Kristia Associates
P.O. Box 1461
Portland, ME 04104

The Majestic Company
Huntington, IN 46750

Superior Fireplace Company
4325 Artesia Ave.
Fullerton, CA 92663

Vestal Manufacturing Co.
Box 420
Sweetwater, TN 37874

Further Readings

If you are interested in fireplaces, you will find many Garden Way books that will be helpful. Here are some of them:

DESIGNING AND BUILDING A SOLAR HOME by Donald Watson. 288 pp., quality paperback, $8.95; cloth, $12.95. Heavily illustrated. Places the solar-heated home in the reach of all of middle America.

THE COMPLETE BOOK OF HEATING WITH WOOD by Larry Gay. 112 pp., quality paperback, $3.95. Practical information for the homeowner.

LOW-COST POLE BUILDING CONSTRUCTION by Douglas Merrilees and Evelyn Loveday. 112 pp., quality paperback, $4.95; cloth, $8.95. Save money, labor, and materials.

LOW-COST SOURCES OF ENERGY FOR THE HOME by Peter Clegg. 250 pp., quality paperback, $5.95; cloth, $8.95. Updated information on alternate energy systems.

These books are available at your bookstore, or may be ordered directly from Garden Way Publishing, Dept. FP, Charlotte, Vermont 05445. If order is less than $10, please add 60¢ postage and handling.

Glossary

Ash dump

The metal opening in the floor of the hearth through which ashes are raked into the ash pit below.

Ash pit

The storage area in the bottom of a chimney where ashes are accumulated under the hearth.

Back hearth

The floor of the fire chamber where the fire is laid.

Breast

That part of the front of the fireplace between the lintel and the throat.

Cap

This refers to certain metal or masonry tops to chimneys.

Cord

A measurement of wood. It refers to a pile of wood 8 feet long by 4 feet wide and 4 feet high, or its equivalent. It is often called a "standard" cord.

Covings

The right and left sides of the fire chamber.

Cricket

A structure built on the up-side of the roof behind and connected to the chimney to prevent rain and ice from accumulating behind the chimney. Also called a **saddle.**

Damper

A metal mechanical sort of dome that fits over the throat of the fireplace and is used to control drafts.

Door to ash pit

A metal door into the ash pit for removal of ashes. This is usually located in the basement or on the outside wall of the chimney.

Face cord

A cord of wood 8 feet long, 4 feet high, and only the depth of a length of firewood. Also called a **short cord, rack,** or **rick.**

Facing

Usually a finish layer of non-combustible material around the top and sides of the fireplace opening.

Fireback

The rear wall of the fire chamber. Usually pertains to the vertical section of the rear wall, while the slanted section is referred to as the **slope of fireback.**

Firebrick

A special hard brick designed for lining the interior of fireplaces where they come in contact with flames.

Fire chamber

The inside of the fireplace where the logs or other fuel are burned.

Fireplace opening

The opening into the fire chamber where fuel is burned.

Firestops

Wood or metal strips to block off open passages to prevent fire from entering.

Flashing

Metal pieces used to form a barrier to prevent moisture from leaking between the chimney and the roof or other woodwork.

Flue

A passage in the chimney for smoke and gases to escape.

Flue liner

A hollow length of vitrified fire clay made to line the inside of flues.

Footing

The foundation for the chimney.

Frame

Usually a border of wood or metal around the outer edges of the fireplace facing.

Front hearth

The extension of the back hearth into the room to provide protection against sparks from the fireplaces.

Hearth

The floor of the fire chamber where the fire is built. It also includes the front hearth although the word "hearth" frequently is used to refer only to the back hearth.

Hood

A flat piece of stone or slate raised on some kind of feet over the top of the flue to prevent unwanted down-drafts, rain, and snow from entering the flue.

Jambs

The front sides of the fireplace opening.

Lintel

A plate of steel or stone across the top of the fireplace opening to support masonry.

Mantel

A sort of shelf above the fireplace, nowadays frequently used to hold decorative articles such as candles and clocks. It may also be part of the frame.

Mortar ties

Strips of soft metal set into the rough masonry against which facing is later attached.

Rack

See **Face cord.**

Raised hearth

This refers to a back hearth and front hearth which are above the level of the floor of the room.

Rick

See **Face cord.**

Saddle

See **Cricket.**

Short cord

See **Face cord.**

Slope of fireback

The slanted section of the fireback.

Smoke chamber

That area above the throat which is reduced in size as it is built upward until it reaches the flue.

Smoke shelf

The horizontal shelf above, and running the length of, the throat. It turns the down-drafts around to prevent them from forcing smoke into the room via the fire chamber.

Spark arrester

A mesh cap on top of the flue to prevent sparks from being carried outside by the up-drafts and to prevent birds and animals from entering the flue.

Subhearth

The foundation for the hearth.

Throat

An opening three to four inches wide running the length of the fire chamber where the breast and slope of fireback otherwise would meet. Smoke and gases from the fire must pass through the throat to get into the flue. The damper rests over the throat.

Wythe

A masonry divider between flues.

Index